T0368264

THE NATURE OF JOY

THE NATURE OF JOY

Alexander B. Platt

with Joanne Dearcopp

This book was printed in the United States of America.

To order additional copies of this book, contact:
Xlibris Corporation
1-888-795-4274
www.Xlibris.com
Orders@Xlibris.com
22817

To my wife, Pat,
our son, Alex, and our daughter, Corinne—
all of whom made a significant contribution
to the evolution of this book.

The most visible joy can only reveal itself to us when we've transformed it, within.

—Rainer Marie Rilke

CONTENTS

ACKNOWLEDGEMENTS

THIS SLENDER BOOK took three and a half years to write and in the process went through nineteen drafts. What I was trying to say was mostly clear to me, but it certainly was not clear to anyone else. It took a heroic effort on the part of Joanne Dearcopp to get me to see that this was my problem and not the fault of my readers. And even when I had finally made that step, she forced me to revisit my ideas over and over again until they were as clear as they were ever going be. She started as an editor but became a muse. If you read and enjoy this book, you owe an awful lot to her.

Others gave various drafts a hard, intensive reading and provided me with lots of critical feedback. Some had serious reservations, but most were encouraging. Many of their suggestions were incorporated into the final text. My bountiful thanks go to Marilyn Button, Bob and Cinny Coulson, Gene Cummiskey, Denny Henkel, Lew Gediman, Jacques Jimenez, and Dick Wedemeyer.

Others read various drafts out of friendly loyalty and a touch of duty. The responses ranged from confusion to incredulity to "so what?", from sympathy for a confused soul to encouragement, and, in the case of my niece, Whitney Meyers, to enthusiastic delight. Positive or not, I found that the feedback was always useful. My grateful thanks go to Peggy Beecher, Kent and Nona Bloomer, my sister, Trevor Campbell, Rose and Gordon Edwards, Judy Gediman, Bob Hart, Whitney Meyers, Bob Moore, Bob Pierson, John and Lynn Sinclair and Fred Yonkman.

My gratitude also to James Wyckoff and Susan Lipsey of the Gurdjieff Foundation, who embody whatever wisdom you find in this book.

INTRODUCTION

BEFORE I BEGIN, I wonder why it is that you have picked up this book to read? You may be interested in joy, as I am, because you want more of it in your life. You may also be intrigued to know what evokes that unique feeling. If you have had moments of intense joy, you may be eager to know what makes them so distinctive and memorable. In this book I attempt to describe the phenomenon of joy and answer the question, What is joy?

Joy, I believe, offers a feeling that is different in quality from other positive life experiences—not just different in degree. There can be different kinds of joy, but I am specifically interested in that fleeting, intense, whole-mind-and-body engagement with a sensory impression resulting from a sequence of changes that can occur when one is in an attentive state, when the body has softened and a sensory experience is absorbed into the body. I explore this process in depth, as I seek to understand why joy is important in our lives.

As a psychologist trained in scientific methodology, I find it difficult to move too far away from hard data. To the best of my knowledge, nothing has been written by social scientists on joy as I define it. Of necessity, I rely heavily on my own personal experiences and observations, and I also include those of others as recorded in fiction, poetry, autobiography, and philosophy. I have encountered descriptive passages in this literature that powerfully capture the feeling and sense of joy I am exploring here, and I include many to illustrate my views. Eastern philosophy and spiritual traditions also inform and support my opinions. The joy I am describing is rooted specifically in sensory awareness, thus some writings (such as those of the Christian mystics who describe joy as a union with God) are not included.

As I take on the role of guide for this exploration of joy, you may be interested in some personal background. Some details I have chosen to include may seem curious at first, but their relevance will become apparent later. Early on, I had to repeat first grade before I was diagnosed as dyslexic and sent to be tutored at a special school in another town. When I came home each day, I did not know any of the local kids and did not play with them. Studying held little interest for me. So, what was there to do? Well, there was a wooded area beside our house with a stream running through it to a pond, and after school I would walk quietly in the woods or sit and simply look and listen. I paid attention to everything. No one told me to do this; it just seemed a natural thing to do. Those times in the woods went on for several years and are still very vivid. Perhaps they were the origins of my later years of meditation.

Your impression thus far may be one of a quiet, inward child. Wrong. I was always a happy-go-lucky goof-off. I loved sports and was a good athlete. Until my sophomore year in college, my number one priority was to have fun and to get into various kinds of mischief. One personality trait—consistent throughout my life, even through the difficulties of being a dyslexic child—has been a basic cheerfulness and optimism.

Many inspiring mentors in my life have supported and fed this inherent optimism. Their encouragement enabled me to overcome dyslexic problems despite professional predictions that I would be best suited as an auto mechanic. The first mentor was Dr. James Leyburn, a professor at Washington and Lee University. He spent a lot of time persuading me that I was smarter than I thought and that I should take college seriously. Eventually I did, though I stopped well short of being a young scholar, instead becoming president of the biggest party house on campus and captain of the football and track teams.

After graduation, I entered the doctoral program in psychology at Columbia University and quickly ran out of money. Arthur Brown, my second significant mentor, was dean of students at Columbia's School of General Studies. He saved me by hiring me to be assistant dean of students, a post that came with free tuition. Equally important, he exposed me to his own expansive, brilliant mind and encouraged a constant exchange of ideas that forced me to stretch my thinking. When Clifford Lord, dean of the School of General Studies, promoted me to replace Brown when he retired, I acquired my third mentor. We would play hooky on a nice afternoon and walk around the city discussing educational issues. His confidence in my ability to be dean of more than five thousand students at the tender age of twenty-six finally convinced me that I could be more than an auto mechanic. Four years later, I became dean of students at Columbia College.

By now I had a Ph. D., a wife, and two children. By the time I met my next mentor, I was focused and goal-oriented, unable to waste a minute, no longer the dreamer of my youth. When Ted Waller, president of Grolier Educational Corporation, had the wit or foolishness to hire a naïve dean to run his Instructional Systems Division, I felt ready for the business world. From Waller I learned how to run a business and manage a national sales organization. I loved to develop new products and to see them sold throughout the country, but I could never really care about business per se.

When I was forty, my wife and I owned a house in the suburbs along with a sailboat and a membership in the local yacht club. This should have been more than enough. However, I was plagued by the questions, "Is this it? or is there more to life than this?" Searching answers to these questions, I joined the Gurdjieff Foundation in New York, and became intensely involved for over twenty years. This was roughly the equivalent of joining a Zen center and committing to its disciplined and rigorous training. At about the same time, I left Grolier and began consulting as a management psychologist to CEOs and their senior executives. My clients ranged from top-one-hundred corporations to small family businesses. I was well paid and was expected to deliver. I had to be practical, focused, goal-oriented, and politically astute. My persona of those years completely masked the seeker.

Then, at the age of sixty, I underwent surgery for prostate cancer. It was a highly aggressive cancer, and there was a period when I was not too sure the surgery would be successful. The effect of this trauma was to prompt a return to reflection and contemplation, during which time I realized that experiences of joy were the source of great meaning in my life. I wanted to understand them. When and why did they occur? Why were they so rare? Were they physical as well as mental? Did they have meaning beyond the momentary experience?

Somewhere in my sixty-fifth year, I felt compelled to write down all that I had concluded about the phenomenon of joy. This discourse on the nature of joy seeks to break new ground and to extend our understanding. If these ideas make sense to you, and I have been able to communicate my understanding of joy, I will have achieved my purpose. If they help you to find more joy in your own life, I will be delighted.

CHAPTER ONE

Positioning Joy

MOST OF US have experienced moments of uncommonly intense vividness that we may have called "joy," but that more likely have gone unnamed. In these experiences we encounter some aspect of the physical world in a way that is direct, immediate, even intimate. The result is a feeling so distinctive and powerful that we know it goes well beyond mere pleasure or delight, a moment of intense contact that involves both mind and body, a moment so memorable we recall it even years later. For just a moment, we are no longer simply situated in the world but instead experience a living connection that seems intensely joyous.

This joy, I believe, is a unique and distinctive phenomenon that results from a process I have tried to analyze into three aspects: attention, softening, and absorption. Joy occurs when a positive sensory impression is absorbed by the body as well as encountered by the mind. The body can absorb a sensory impression only when it has softened because the mind is attentive to the stimulus. The ultimate effect is that, for a moment, our body and mind become continuous with the world. As Zen teachers describe it, we have attained a moment of nonseparation, a moment of intimacy with the world. There is no awareness of one's self as separate from the sensory stimuli absorbed. One experiences this as joy.

In this book, I will describe how I believe the process leading to joy occurs. To do so, I bring together evidence I have accumulated from my training and experience as a psychologist, my lifelong love of literature and study of religion and philosophy, and my experience with meditation. I hope to convince you that joy is a distinct psychophysical experience, potentially available to everyone.

Definition

When moments of joy come and go, what follows is usually a sense of wonder. What was that? Where did it come from? Why is it different from other pleasurable experiences? Before exploring the nature of joy, let us first define and distinguish the experience of joy from that of pleasure, delight, or happiness.

If we look in numerous dictionaries, we can see that words such as "pleasure," "happiness," and "enjoyment," "delight" and "satisfaction," "joy" and "ecstasy" are used interchangeably. Only the 1967 unabridged edition of the *Random House Dictionary of the English Language* makes some distinctions under the general term "pleasure":

> PLEASURE, ENJOYMENT, DELIGHT, JOY refer to the feeling of being pleased and happy. PLEASURE is the general term: *to take pleasure in beautiful scenery*. ENJOYMENT is a quiet sense of well-being and pleasurable satisfaction: *enjoyment at sitting in the shade on a warm day*. DELIGHT is a high degree of pleasure, usually leading to active expression of it. JOY is a feeling of delight so deep and so lasting that one radiates happiness and expresses it spontaneously.

These distinctions provide a good starting point for those made later in this book. We find these distinctions expressed in literature, with clear detail and certainty. Joy is described as an experience with a different quality from that of pleasure or delight. Literature confirms my belief in the distinctiveness of joy and my definition of it as an intense whole-mind-and-body feeling.

Context

The field of positive psychology, in the last decade or so, has begun to examine the subjects of happiness, subjective well-being, and pleasure. It has not, however, recognized joy as a distinct psychological experience. Those who have written about the more generalized states of well-being and happiness use a variety of terms such as "pleasure," "ecstasy," and "joy" interchangeably to describe these positive feelings.

It is useful to relate "joy" as I define it to the writings of two of the more eminent authors on positive psychology: Dr. Martin Seligman, in *Authentic Happiness*, and Dr. Mihaly Csikszentmihalyi in *Flow: The Psychology of Optimal Experience*. Dr. Seligman describes the field of positive psychology as including the study of both positive feelings (such as ecstasy, joy, and comfort) and positive activities that have no feeling component at all (such as total engagement). In the context of this scheme, the joy I am describing is in the category of feelings and can be positioned within the context of positive psychology.

Another contextual distinction that may be helpful is joy versus "flow," as described by Dr. Csikszentmihalyi. While some individuals might feel they have experienced joy after a flow experience, it is not the joy I am describing. Flow is the use of one's skills and abilities as a sustained response to an optimal challenge. Let me give an example. A mountaineer is scaling a cliff that challenges his ability. His attention is riveted on where to climb next, and he has lost all sense of time and himself. He is in a state of flow. When he reaches the top, he feels the elation of achieving the goal and a flood of emotions related to his mastery and achievement. He may use the word "joy" to describe this flood of emotions, but these emotions are also not the joy I define and present in this book.

There are considerable similarities in the different processes that result in each. However, the difference between flow and joy is that flow comes from focused attention on a skilled activity aimed at reaching a goal, whereas joy is the result of one's attention being focused on a sensory impression for its own sake.

Sensory Joy

All the examples of joy that I explore here are based on direct sensory impressions. They are not the result of a thought or an idea. It could well be that I am describing only a certain kind of joy, a joy based upon sensory experience. People speak of the joy they experience when they win a long-coveted award or when they learn a grandchild has been born. These are certainly happy occasions, but they are more of a very pleasing mental event than a direct, sensory experience.

In the canon of Christian literature there is a wide spectrum of experiences described as "joy." This feeling may result from doing the will of God, from knowing there is a God, from having made contact through prayer, or from union with God. But none is the result of absorbing a direct sensory impression.

Different Dimension

Although I believe joy is at the upper end of a continuum of gradations of positive feelings similar to that suggested by the *Random House Dictionary*, it is also a unique phenomenon. On a distinctly different dimension from the general well-being of "happiness," joy introduces us to a feeling of great intimacy and connectedness with our world that can profoundly alter how we view our very nature. When we experience joy, we question whether the way we encounter the world in our ordinary, everyday state is the only way. Exploring the nature of joy has convinced me that there are dimensions of our human nature that are not generally recognized and understood in Western psychology. I believe a better understanding of the feeling of joy can lead us to a fuller conception of ourselves and expand the potential we have to enrich our lives.

While we all recognize that joy is entirely spontaneous and unpredictable, it is my observation that there is an identifiable sequence of events and changes that precede that experience. In this book I present my understanding of the process that leads to joy—a sequence that begins with a mental attentiveness to some sensory impression, followed by a softening of the body, which in turn leads to the absorption of the sensory impression by the body. I will explore each of these elements in depth, in order to provide a new understanding of the nature of joy.

CHAPTER TWO

Attention

"ATTENTION" IS THE first element in the process that culminates in joy. As you try to understand this difficult subject, I suggest you forgo attempting a clear, analytical understanding of attention, and that you focus instead on the literary passages I have included here. They will begin to give you a good feel for the subject.

Joy is inherently spontaneous and involuntary, but there are factors that greatly increase the probability of its occurring. One is the nature and degree of one's attention. One's attentiveness can transform perception of a sensory impression in such a way that it leads to joy. Sensory impressions that lead to joy do so only on certain occasions. What makes an occasion special has something to do with the quality of perception of the person receiving the sensory impressions. I will attempt to establish what it is that can lead to an enhanced quality of perception, and the role that attention plays in all this.

We may be only peripherally aware of an object or we may consciously choose to attend to it. In either case, the quality of our attending will affect the quality of our perceiving. For example, you see a lovely maple tree. If you are in a hurry, in a frenzied state with a hundred thoughts rumbling around in your mind, you will know perhaps that the tree is there, but you will not really see it. If you were to take a minute to quiet down, you would experience actually seeing the tree. You would notice its beauty in detail. The quality of your attention directly affects the richness of your perception of the tree. The quality of our perception is a direct function of the quality of our attention, so we must be concerned with the qualitative differences in attention.

Quality

Attention has long been the subject of interest for academic psychology, which has focused on the selectiv-

ity of perception, the voluntary control over this se-
lectivity, and capacity limits in mental functioning. The
dominant model used today in the study of attention
is information processing; indeed, there are some who
question whether the concept of attention is neces-
sary at all. This may be an appropriate question with
regard to our ordinary attention, but what academic
psychologists have not recognized is that there are
qualitative differences in attention. Consider, for example, the difference between someone slicing a car-
rot by rote versus one attending to the task. The former
may be thinking ahead to the table setting and might
manage to get the pieces in the pot while their mind
has not ever attended to what they are doing. The
person attentive to the task will feel the texture, note
the aroma, engage in the movement of the knife in
order to slice attractive, even slices. They are each
performing the task but with a noticeable contrast in
attentiveness.

To introduce the notion of qualitative differences
in attention, I would like to refer to the psychologist
Dr. Abraham Maslow who wrote about "total attention," which occurs when something is exclusively and
entirely attended to. Maslow contends that, in normal perceiving, the object is in effect filtered through
one's mental apparatus and the percept (what one is
seeing) becomes a concept or category. "Total atten-

tion" occurs when attention is given exclusively to the figure, as opposed to the ground or the context in which the figure is situated. The figure generally has form or structure and appears to be in front of the ground. In figure-ground terminology, the figure is the object of focus and the ground is the rest of the perceptual field. Maslow goes on to say that, when one's attention is given exclusively to the figure, it is as though the percept has become for the moment the whole of Being. The percept is no longer regarded or perceived as a member of one category or another but is seen for itself in all its freshness. Another way to consider this is that what is perceived has been totally absorbed without any filtering or conditioning—or at least with less filtering or conditioning.

While Maslow's "total attention" is one way of describing a qualitatively different kind of attention, it is not the only way. The author Annie Dillard describes another very unique kind of attention in her Pulitzer Prize-winning book *Pilgrim at Tinker Creek*. She speaks neither of total attention nor of the figure/ground analogy where one focuses on a single thing to the exclusion of all the rest. Instead, Dillard describes yet another way of perceiving that consists of "letting go." When she walks with her camera, she tells us, she uses her head to see, but when she is without a camera, she registers what is out there in a very different way:

Seeing is of course very much a matter of verbalization. Unless I call my attention to what passes before my eyes, I simply won't see it. It is, as Ruskin says, "Not merely unnoticed, but in the full, clear sense of the word, unseen." My eyes alone can't solve the analogy tests using figures, the ones which show with increasing elaborations, a big square, then a small square in a big square, then a big triangle, and expect me to find a small triangle in a big triangle. I have to say the words, describe what I am seeing. If Tinker Mountain erupted, I'd be likely to notice. But if I want to notice the lesser cataclysms of valley life, I have to maintain in my head a running description of the present. It's not that I'm observant; it's just that I talk too much. Otherwise, especially in a strange place, I'll never know what is happening. Like a blind man at the ball game, I need a radio. When I see this way I analyze and pry. I hurl over logs and roll away stones; I study the bank a square foot at a time, probing and tilting my head. Some days when a mist covers the mountains, when the muskrats won't show and the microscope's mirror shatters, I want to climb up the blank

> blue dome as a man would storm the in-
> side of a circus tent, wildly dangling, and
> with a steel knife claw a rent in the top,
> peep, and, if I must, fall.
> But there is another way of seeing that in-
> volves letting go. When I see this way I
> sway transfixed and emptied. The differ-
> ence between the two ways of seeing is the
> difference between walking with and with-
> out a camera. When I walk with a camera I
> walk from shot to shot, reading the light
> on a calibrated meter. When I walk with-
> out a camera, my own shutter opens, and
> the moment's light prints on my own sil-
> ver gut. When I see this second way I am
> above all an unscrupulous observer.

Annie Dillard perceives the world in a special way when she is letting go. She is consciously paying attention and actively attending to the whole of her environment in a manner quite different from what we think of as ordinary paying attention.

Normal attention comes and goes in spite of ourselves. This not something we do, but something that happens to us. Our mind attends to this and then to that. If we try to pay attention to something, soon our eye wanders to something else or our mind veers to a stray thought. I am not referring to inattention but to our ordinary attention. This normal attention shifts to a more focused attention either when we are surprised by a stimulus and then attend to it directly or else when we consciously decide to focus intently on something. I refer to the first case as "captured attention," and the second case as "active attention."

Captured Attention

When we encounter something extraordinarily captivating, we become highly attentive to it. It is as if our attention has been "captured" and we have no choice but to heed the stimulus. Captured attention is involuntary, but the degree of our alertness and receptivity to such moments or stimuli can determine the likelihood of our responding.

In his short story, "The Second Tree from the Corner," author E. B. White describes a special moment of joy during a rather trying period in the life of his lead character. The character, Mr. Trexler, has been meeting with a psychiatrist. During their fifth session, the doctor asks, "What do you want?" with special emphasis on the word want. Trexler replies, "I don't know. I guess nobody knows the answer to that one." "Sure they do," replies the doctor. The doctor knows what he himself wants: a wing on the small house he owns in Westport, and the money and leisure to do the things he wants to do. At the end of the session, Trexler walks dizzily through the empty waiting room, steps into the street, and turns west toward Madison Avenue in New York City:

> It was an evening of clearing weather, the
> Park showing green and desirable in the
> distance, the last daylight applying a high
> lacquer to the brick and brownstone walls
> and giving the street scene a luminous and
> intoxicating splendor. Trexler meditated,
> as he walked, on what he wanted. "What
> do you want?" he heard again. Trexler
> knew what he wanted, and what, in gen-
> eral, all men wanted; and he was glad, in a
> way, that it was both inexpressible and
> unattainable, and that it wasn't a wing.
> He was satisfied to remember that it was
> deep, formless, enduring, and impossible
> of fulfillment, and that it made men sick,
> and that when you sauntered along Third
> Avenue and looked through the doorways
> into the dim saloons, you could sometimes
> pick out from the unregenerate ranks the
> ones who had not forgotten, gazing
> steadily into the bottom of their glasses on
> the long chance that they could get another

little peek at it. Trexler found himself renewed by the remembrance that what he wanted was at once great and microscopic, and that although it borrowed from the nature of large deeds and of youthful love and of old songs and early intimations, it was not one of these things, and that it had not been isolated and pinned down, and that a man who attempted to define it in the privacy of a doctor's office would fall flat on his face.

Trexler felt invigorated. Suddenly his sickness seemed health, his dizziness stability. A small tree, rising between him and the light, stood there saturated with the evening, each gilt-edged leaf perfectly drunk with excellence and delicacy. Trexler's spine registered an ever so slight tremor as it picked up this natural disturbance in the lovely scene. "I want the second tree from the corner, just as it stands," he said, answering an imaginary question from an imaginary physician. He felt a slow pride in realizing that what he wanted none could bestow, and that what he had none could take away. He felt content to be sick, unembarrassed at being afraid; and in the jungle of his fear he glimpsed (as he had so often glimpsed them before) the flashy tail feathers of the bird of courage.

The luminous and intoxicating evening clearly had an impact on Trexler, and his spine even registered the disturbance of the small tree of which each leaf was "drunk with excellence." There is little question that Trexler's attention was captured by the scene and that he experienced something very powerful and profound, something I am going to call "joy," even though White does not use that word.

When something in our environment captures our attention, we respond almost always by paying even closer attention to it. It is usually the case that the closer we pay attention to something, the more interesting it becomes, with the result that we pay even closer attention. As a result, a self-reinforcing action is established, intensifying the level of attention. There seems to be a connection between one's attention being captured and a subsequent powerful experience.

Personal Experience

To further clarify the connection between captured attention and a powerful experience that might be called joy, let me describe a few of these still-very-much-alive memories from my youth where captured attention triggered a joy experience. For several summers during my adolescence, I was lucky enough to be a crewmember on an ocean-racing sailboat. I was competitive, but what I really loved was to be on night watch. If the sails were set and the course was steady, I would just sit and absorb the beauty of the evening. The light of the moon would scatter across the waves. Sailing through beds of phosphorus, the boat would leave a long, glowing trail. There was the sound of the breeze and the steady motion of the boat as it cut through the water. All else was quiet. I absorbed the night. I mean that in both a metaphorical and a literal sense (I hope to explain this adequately, as we go along).

Here is another memory. After serving my military obligation, I had a three-month break before returning to graduate school. With several friends I bummed around Europe, and we arrived one day in Heidelberg where it was our intention to find some student hangouts and drink vast quantities of beer, which we did. One evening I wandered off alone and ended up at the cathedral, in the town square, where there happened to be an all-Bach concert. To my surprise, the chamber orchestra was located on a platform up in the rafters of the cathedral. The audience sat below. The acoustics were extraordinary, and I have never forgotten the penetrating sounds of Bach's music descending from the heavens. No thoughts, no analysis—my body was the music. I can still experience the touch of a similar joy, on occasion, when listening to Bach.

On another occasion, one Saturday during my first year of graduate school, I was walking around the city and noticed the New York City Ballet. I knew nothing about ballet and had never seen it performed. I bought a ticket, attended that evening, and was captivated by what I saw—Balanchine's new ballets "Agon" and "Apollo," both performed by Jacques D'Amboise. My senses were deluged. Even though a varsity athlete, I had no idea the human body could move like that or join with a partner in such graceful complexity. I found the beauty of the movement overwhelming.

In each of these three experiences, my attention was caught by extraordinary visual and auditory stimuli. I was so captured by the stimuli that I in turn paid even more attention. There was a spiraling effect, and then something happened. The experience changed in quality. I was physically affected. Even today, many years later, those experiences are still vivid—I remember them in my body, not just with my mind. These experiences were fundamentally different from the ordinary pleasurable experiences of life.

Active Attention

If you wish to pursue more joyful experiences, you will not want to rely on captured attention, because you will be relying on chance. Rather, you will want to develop the ability to actively attend to an object as an act of will. By learning to deliberately be more attentive, you can take a first step toward experiencing more joy.

In order to convey a better sense of active attention, I suggest that you try the following experiment. Tomorrow morning, when you are sipping your coffee or tea, try to bring the cup to your lips with intention, sip from it, then put it down. Make each movement one you consciously *will* rather than one that just happens. See how long you can do this before your mind wanders and you just automatically bring the cup to your lips. Now try the experiment again, but this time deliberately taste the contents. Be attentive to the taste during the time you actually drink. Then, with attention, put the cup down.

You will find that you cannot do the above exercise for very long. You cannot do it because you are not sufficiently attentive. A myriad of thoughts invade your attention—what you forgot to do yesterday, what you must do today—and your focus is lost. If your coffee or tea tasted like something else, you would notice it, but otherwise you really do not taste it. So how can it give you pleasure?

If we were really able to be attentive, the first thing we observed would be the continual chatter going on in our minds. We talk to ourselves continually, and in so doing we create and maintain our world. I am sure most of you have at one time or another watched yourselves mentally. You are no doubt aware of the way you think by chance association, one thought leading to another. Typically, something new captures your interest and instantly makes you forget what was preoccupying you the moment before. We become identified with each new interest or thought, and it is this identification that keeps us locked into the contents of our mind, and closed to what is right here, right now. It is only by being attentive to what is here, now, that we have a chance of experiencing joy.

If we observe the contents of our minds (and we are always preoccupied by that content), it is clear that we are typically either justifying or enjoying events of the past or anticipating the future with either pleasure or concern. We are living in the past or future, neither of which actually exists. The only thing that does exist is each moment, the present, even though we seldom live there. The ever-changing content of our mind is like a box in which we live, sealed off from the potential vividness of reality. And even when we experience something strong or significant, our mind begins to talk about it, to label it and analyze it, and the experience is lost.

It is not surprising that some of the authors I draw on who describe joy and joy-like experiences also speak to the subject of attention, alertness, and awakeness. C. S. Lewis, in *Surprised by Joy*, wrote:

> Only when your whole attention and desire are fixed on something else—whether a distant mountain, or the past, or the Gods of Asgard—does the "thrill" arise. It is a by-product. Its very existence presupposes that you desire not it but something other and outer.

And Thoreau, in *Walden*, put it this way:

> We must learn to reawaken and keep ourselves awake, not by mechanical aids, but by an infinite expectation of the dawn, which does not forsake in our soundest sleep. I know of no more encouraging fact than the unquestionable ability of man to elevate his life by a conscious endeavor. It is something to be able to paint a particular picture, or to carve a statue, and so make a few objects beautiful; but it is far more glorious to carve and paint the very atmosphere and medium through which we look, which morally we can do.

These literary examples describe well the connection between active attention, or as Thoreau put it, "alertness," and the quality of our perception. We have seen also that there seems to be a connection between this quality of perception and the experience we are calling joy. (In the next chapter we will look into the underlying factors that facilitate this connection and see that both active and captured attention have the effect of softening the body.)

Quiet Mind

Active attention also has the important effect of quieting the mind, allowing it to be more receptive to stimuli. The Zen Master John Daido Loori, Roshi, speaks of an attention in which the mind is unobstructed—always open and receptive. Daido Roshi, in *The Still Point,* wrote of zazen or meditation and of the underlying stillness of active attention:

> Every other creature on the face of the earth seems to know how to be quiet and still. A butterfly on a leaf, a cat in front of a fireplace; even a hummingbird comes to rest sometime. But humans are constantly on the go. We seem to have lost the ability to

just be quiet, to simply be present in the stillness that is the foundation of our lives. Yet, if we never get in touch with that stillness, we never fully experience our lives.

When the mind is at rest, the body is at rest—respiration, heartbeat and metabolism slow down. Reaching this still point is not something unusual or esoteric. It is a very important part of being alive and staying awake. All creatures on the earth manifest this stillness.

In zazen, as you practice letting go of your thoughts and internal dialogue, and bringing your mind back to the breath, the breath will slowly get easier and deeper, and the mind will naturally rest. The mind is like the surface of a pond. When the wind blows, the surface is disturbed. Then there are waves and ripples, and the image of the sun or the moon is broken up.

When the wind quiets down, the surface of the pond becomes like glass. The stilled mind is like a mirror. It doesn't process, it just reflects . . . A still mind is unobstructed—always open and receptive. It doesn't hold on or attach to anything. At any moment in time, it is free.

You yourself may have already noticed that, when you become more attentive, the inner dialogue and the flow of images begin to slow down. To see this more clearly, here is another exercise you can try right now. In the course of the day, we all go through a series of postures that are characteristic of ourselves. This is a particularly interesting exercise because many of our postures are often correlated with a distinct emotional state, and if you study yourself long enough, you will be able to know pretty well what emotional state you are in by observing your posture. First, notice the posture you are in right now. Now sense your body in that posture. What does that posture feel like? Get to know your body in that posture. Stop reading for a few minutes and be attentive.

Did you notice that while you were paying attention to your body there were not as many thoughts coming and going in your mind and that what thoughts there were really did not get in your way? They came and went, but you were being attentive elsewhere. Similarly, when one is attentive and quiet of mind, sensory impressions need not battle to get past the obstacles and noise that generally prevail in one's mind. They can be felt more fully, particularly if the body has softened as a consequence of a change in attention.

CHAPTER THREE

Softening

T HE HEAD OR the mind lives either in the past or in the future. Only the body lives in the present. And since joy occurs totally in the present, the body is essential to this experience. Being attentive is not only a way of quieting the mind to enhance receptivity of a stimulus, it is also a way of softening the body and enabling one to enter the body, occupy it, and be present. The softening effect of attention allows the body to absorb a sensory impression directly and to feel it fully. Only through this physical change in the body—a softening, so to speak—is one able to experience joy.

How do we know the body "softens"? Well, most of us know there can be great differences in how we feel and express ourselves. There are times when we can be abrupt, hard, impervious, and insensitive. At other times, we can feel softer and more porous, when we can manifest ourselves as receptive, responsive, sensitive, and open. Circumstances, even our thoughts, can change or move us in one direction or the other. In a business setting among strong-minded peers, we may be tough. At home in the evening with our spouse or children, we may be more sensitive. Some may like being hardened and may feel a little awkward or embarrassed to soften. Others may actually prefer to be more sensitive but may project a harder self as a mask. And some may like being both. Normally, we do not feel the change in the quality of our being; we are seldom aware of the transition. If we were more aware, we might sense the difference in our bodies.

Many people are so formed as a consequence of their life circumstances that they never change, or perhaps they move only slightly from being very hard to less hard. Others move in the other direction—from being generally soft and porous to somewhat less so. Many oscillate quietly in a middle range, while others swing dramatically from one extreme to the other. The last are, of course, the most noticeable.

To give you a sense of what I mean by a softening of the body, recall a time when you were very much in love, and your partner was equally in love with you. Remember an occasion when the two of you were alone together and totally in sync. Perhaps you were taking a walk or having a picnic. Remember how the two of you just flowed together. No bumps, no edges. You did not have to think about what to do—the two of you were like one person, completely harmonious, relaxed and at ease. Now think of an occasion when you had just had a bitter argument with your partner, and you were still together in the same room. If you could go back and feel your body on those two occasions, you would find that on the first it was soft while on the second it was hard.

Do the terms "soft" and "hard" refer to anything more than the tensing and relaxing of the muscles in the body? Perhaps not. There are those who would say that, when we are soft, the energy in our body is flowing freely, whereas when we are tense, the energy is frozen. But even without the concept of energy, the levels of muscular tension in our bodies go far deeper and are more complex than we normally realize. I prefer to use the terms "hard" and "soft" rather than "tense" and "relaxed" to describe the state of one's body and demeanor.

Attention and Softening

It is my belief that when a person becomes more attentive, the body softens. To see an example of this effect, let us look at a passage from Melville's *Moby Dick* that implies a softening, even for Ahab, a most unlikely candidate:

> It was a clear steel-blue day. The firmaments of air and sea were hardly separable in that all-pervading azure; only, the pensive air was transparently pure and soft, with a woman's look, and the robust and man-like sea heaved with long, strong, lingering swells, as Samson's chest in his sleep . . . Tied up and twisted; gnarled and knotted with wrinkles; haggardly and unyielding; his eyes glowing like coals, that still glow in the ashes of ruin; untottering Ahab stood forth in the clearness of the morn; lifting his splintered helmet of a brow to the fair girl's forehead of heaven.
> Slowly crossing the deck from the scuttle, Ahab leaned over the side, and watched how his shadow in the water sank and sank to his gaze, the more and the more that he strove to pierce the profundity. But

the lovely aromas in that enchanted air did at last seem to dispel, for a moment, the cankerous thing in his soul. That glad, happy air, that winsome sky, did at last stroke and caress him; the step-mother world, so long cruel—forbidding—now threw affectionate arms around his stubborn neck, and did seem joyously to sob over him, as if over one, that however willful and erring, she could yet find it in her heart to save and bless. From beneath his slouched hat Ahab dropped a tear into the sea; nor did all the Pacific contain such wealth as that one wee drop.

Ahab—driven and unbending, willing to sacrifice anything and anyone in pursuit of the white whale—suddenly softens and drops a tear in the sea. Melville no doubt attributed this change to the effects of the "clear steel-blue day." He wrote, "But the lovely aromas in that enchanted air did at last seem to dispel, for a moment, the cankerous thing in his soul." However, when Ahab "watched how his shadow in the water sank and sank to his gaze, the more and the more that he strove to pierce the profundity," his attention was captured. As he strove to "pierce the profundity," he had no choice but to be in a state of intense alertness—

concentration, or what I prefer to call attention—and he softened.

Another literary example, or poetic metaphor, of the softening effect of attention can be seen in act 5, scene 1, of Shakespeare's *Merchant of Venice*, where Lorenzo notes the effects of music on youthful, unhandled colts. The colts are captured by sounds of music and their "savage eyes turned to a modest gaze":

Jessica
I am never merry when I hear sweet music.

Lorenzo
The reason is your spirits are attentive,
For do but note a wild and wanton herd
Or race of youthful and unhandled colts
Fetching mad bounds, bellowing and neighing
    loud,
Which is the hot condition of their blood;
If they but hear perchance a trumpet sound,
Or any air of music touch their ears,
You shall perceive them make a mutual stand,
Their savage eyes turned to a modest gaze
By the sweet power of music. Therefore the
    poet
Did feign that Orpheus drew trees, stones,
    and floods,

Since naught so stockish, hard, and full of rage,
But music for the time doth change his nature.
The man who has no music in himself,
Nor is not moved with concord of sweet
   sounds,
Is fit for treasons, stratagems and spoils;
The motions of his spirit are dull as night,
And his affections as dark as Erebus.
Let no such man be trusted. Mark the music.

The sweet music has the effect of producing what I would call a softening effect on the unhandled colts.

To the best of my knowledge there is no empirical data to support this cause-and-effect relationship between attentiveness and the body's softening. However, from my own experience, and that of others I have talked with, the relationship does exist. I hope that from your own personal experience you will agree that what I am saying seems intuitively right.

Remember also what John Daido Loori wrote earlier: "When the mind is at rest, the body is at rest—respiration, heart beat and metabolism slow down. Reaching this still point is not something unusual or esoteric. It is a very important part of being alive and staying awake. All creatures on the earth manifest this stillness." When the mind is at rest, the body softens. When we are mentally agitated, the body hardens.

We may not realize it, but our bodies react to the thoughts that pass through our minds. Since so many of our thoughts are worries or concerns about what is going on in our lives, or nervous anticipations of what we face in the future, it is not surprising that various parts of our body become tense and remain that way. Think of what happens when something frightens you. You catch your breath and your body tenses. This is what is happening all the time on a less dramatic and more subtle level. Exercise, laughter, and love can soften those tensions for a while, but they soon return. And I refer not just to the obvious tensions in the neck and shoulders. There are seemingly endless levels of tension we never realize are there until we begin the work of softening the body through meditation.

An Exercise

Now let me give you a personal example of how this softening may be achieved. I sit, close my eyes, and bring my attention to my body. As I do this, I am able to sense my entire organism—to experience the sensation of every part of my body. At first, I can sense only one part of my body at a time, but in due course I can sense my entire body simultaneously. As I work with the attention in my body, there proceeds in me a struggle—the struggle to keep my attention on my body rather to get caught by random thoughts and reactions. As these thoughts and reactions diminish and my attention becomes stronger, I begin to move it around my body and inevitably encounter areas of tension, areas that are closed or dead rather than open and vibrant. As I encounter these areas, there proceeds a second struggle, which is to have those parts relax. These struggles occur because I am consciously thinking, "relax the leg" and as a result, I am inevitably separated from my leg.

However, there comes a moment, spontaneous and involuntary, when I have internal silence. Now I am in a state of pure attention. My body softens, hardens partially, and then softens again. I do not *do* anything. In this state, I no longer observe my body. Rather, I *am* my body. One experiences this softening of the body as its natural state, the state it would exist in were it not for the tensions that generally permeate it.

When I slowly open my eyes and look around the room, keeping some of the attention on my body while giving some of my attention to the room, the state of my body changes. It is not as soft anymore. If I speak, dividing my attention between my body and my speaking, I notice that my legs begin to close up somewhat, and if I start to move, there is a slight tension in my hips and lower back. Then, I lose my attention completely and get caught up in whatever I am saying or doing. When I come back to myself, I see that my body has become closed, hard, and tense, at least relatively speaking.

Effects of Softening

When we are tense and hard, we react automatically to every stimulus as it comes our way. This just seems to be a part of our nature. On a moment-to-moment basis, we react to a stimulus either physically (including an inner tensing), emotionally, or with our head (a mental thought or image). We then react to our reaction. All of this happens so quickly that normally we are unaware of it. Our reaction is completely automatic and determined by our biological disposition, cultural background, and training. On a broader basis, however, we do have some degree of freedom, because we can often anticipate the consequences of our possible action and behave accordingly.

Whenever the body softens, we respond differently to stimuli; we no longer react so automatically. As our body softens, it is returning to its more natural state, less encumbered by our conditioning, and thus more able to respond directly to stimuli. We no longer react automatically and exclusively with our mind but, rather, are able to respond to the particular present situation within our body as well. This organic integrated response of both the body and mind together is "feeling." On the other hand, a purely automatic response triggered by what we think, based on our life's conditioning and our perception of the immediate circumstance within that context, is "emotion." That knee-jerk emotional response actually serves to separate us from the essential substance of what we are reacting to; it is a fending off rather than an incorporation of the stimulus. Feeling can be very strong, so strong that at times we can hardly tolerate it. To feel is to bear something. Consider how much more difficult it is to bear the negative impressions of another person rather than to react emotionally to them. Yet consider also the intensity of a positive feeling that one is open to when the body has softened.

Our thinking also changes when we are in a softer state. We understand, but not with our typical linear, associative thinking. The structures and categories we use to perceive the world become more flexible and less exclusive. Categories break down. For example, in our everyday state we may assume that a "tough" person is just that and cannot also be "gentle," or vice versa. In an attentive state, we no longer find that one category or concept precludes others. Once our preconceived notions are less entrenched, we are able to see a person as possibly both gentle and tough. Our conditioning becomes less influential on how we perceive a stimulus. This allows us a broader perspective, and we are more sensitive to context rather than preconceived categories. We are less driven by the ego. We see new ways of understanding or approaching an issue or situation rather than relying on old ideas.

Finally, when we are in a softer state, the way we hold our body and the way we move both change. People who have spent years meditating tend to have motions and gestures that are very smooth. When they sit, they are simply in a state of repose. There is little tension in their body, so they move in a way that is simple and appropriate to whatever they are doing. There is no extraneous motion, no jerkiness, and most assuredly, no rushing. They move differently not because they have a different physical structure but because they move with little tension; they move as their bodies were made to move.

I have described three significant consequences of our body softening: how we feel, how we think, and how we move. There is yet another consequence that is far less understood. It is experienced only by those who, either by chance or by deliberate effort, have brought themselves to a high level of attentiveness. In this state they experience being able to absorb sensory impressions. What is actually happening here no one knows, including myself, but from my personal experience it feels as if I am being touched, even nourished by what I am attending to at the moment. Many will assume that "absorption of an impression" is just a metaphor, but I hope to explain why I am convinced that it is a specific, identifiable phenomenon.

CHAPTER FOUR

Absorption

EITHER WE ARE attentive to begin with or some sensory object captures our attention, or some combination of these two situations occurs. As we become more attentive (which is often but not always the case), the constant talk in our head quiets down and our body begins to soften as a consequence. With inner talk slowed down and the body softer, we are now better able to feel or, as I like to put it, "absorb" into our bodies a sensory stimulus. It is when the body absorbs such a stimulus that the scales tip from delight to joy. I believe that absorption is the key to joy. Why is this so? Because it is the absorption that puts the body into a seamless connection with the source of the sensory impression. Joy is this profound connectedness, a sense of "one-ness," devoid of all thought. It is not something you think about—it just happens.

There is an important distinction to be made between my use of the term "absorption" and the way it is used by two other psychologists who write on the subject of positive psychology. Both Seligman and Csikszentmihalyi use the word "absorption" to mean being so fully engaged in an activity that for the time of that engagement you forget about yourself. I use the word to describe a phenomenon whereby a sensory impression is taken into the body as well as the mind.

Reacting or Absorbing

To assimilate or absorb a sensory impression into our organism is profoundly different from simply registering or reacting to such a stimulus. To assimilate an impression is, in a sense, to absorb its energy, not just into the head but also into the body. The sensory experience becomes a part of our person.

I believe the philosopher Maurice Merleau-Ponty described this kind of absorption. He stated in *The*

Primacy of Perception, "To perceive is to render oneself present to something through the body." To be present to something is to be available to it, to absorb it, not just to register it or react to it.

It is important to understand, and indeed feel, the difference in oneself between merely reacting to a stimulus and absorbing that stimulus. I have already described the softening effects of attention and the differences between emotion and feeling. I wrote that "emotion" is an internal, virtually automatic reaction to a stimulus, governed by our conditioning, education, and genes. We are separated from what we are reacting to by our reaction itself, which is the emotion. In contrast, "feeling" is an organic, sweeping, body experience accompanied by a perception of this experience in the mind. To feel is to truly receive a stimulus with one's entire organism. The distinction between emotion and feeling is not much discussed in contemporary psychology, but it must be made in order to understand the nature of joy. In *Looking for Spinoza: Joy, Sorrow, and the Feeling Brain*, the neurologist Antonio Damasio also makes this distinction between emotion and feeling. Joy is a feeling, not an emotion.

One reason we so rarely experience joy is that in our everyday lives we continually react to the world around us rather than absorb it. An event occurs, and although we could truly feel and absorb the impression of the event, this is rarely the case. Instead, we react to the event, and our reactions are based upon the ideas, categories, and concepts that we have developed and solidified over the years. When reacting to an event, all we experience is our reaction. The event itself is no longer felt.

Here is a personal example of how this short-circuiting of an initial impression occurs. It was a situation in which many of us could have experienced feelings of true sadness, but instead we just underwent an emotional response. My wife and I were sitting at dinner on a cruise ship when it was announced that one of the group had left her table, gone to her cabin, pushed the emergency button, and died. This being a university-sponsored trip, we all knew this attractive and friendly lady, to one extent or another. The volume of conversation in the dining room was always quite high, as it had been just prior to the announcement. After the announcement, there was a brief moment of stunned silence, and then the noise level of the conversation returned to the same volume.

At my table people were asking each other, "What could she have died of?" "Did she look okay when you last saw her?" "Where is her husband?" "How old are her children?" and so on. The conversational back and forth continued through the rest of dinner.

Absorption • 65

No one was experiencing the initial impression of the event. A human being known to all of us had just died, suddenly, just like that. The group reacted by becoming preoccupied with their questions and speculations and information gathering. The reaction of the group could well be seen as an elaborate effort to avoid feeling the pain or great sadness of such a close brush with death. Real feeling is very strong, and we tend to avoid it. As a consequence, we rarely fully experience our interaction with the world in general, and with people in particular. Unfortunately, we almost always react—and then experience our reaction—rather than experience the event or impression that prompted the reaction.

Dynamics of Absorption

In literature we find the most persuasive evidence to support my belief that when the mind is attentive and the body quiet, thoroughly relaxed and softened, sensory impressions are absorbed into the body and one's whole being. The following excerpts give insight into the dynamics of how and under what circumstances absorption occurs, and its role in the process of joy. For example, in *Walden,* Thoreau described what I am calling absorption when he wrote:

I did not read books the first summer; I hoed beans. Nay, I often did better than this. There were times when I could not afford to sacrifice the bloom of the present moment to any work, whether of the head or hands. I love a broad margin to my life. Sometimes, in a summer morning, having taken my accustomed bath, I sat in my sunny doorway from sunrise till noon, rapt in a revery, amidst the pines and hickories and sumacs, in undisturbed solitude and stillness, while the birds sang around or flitted noiseless through the house, until by the sun falling in at my west window or the noise of some traveller's wagon on the distant highway, I was reminded of the lapse of time. I grew in those seasons like corn in the night, and they were far better than any work of the hands would have been. They were not time subtracted from my life, but so much over and above my usual allowance.

I do not believe that Thoreau was being metaphorical when he wrote, "I grew in the seasons like corn in the night." Instead, he intuited that he was absorbing the impressions of his surroundings, and he called that process "growing." Further, he acknowledges the richness of his time spent in stillness.

In *Pilgrim at Tinker Creek*, Annie Dillard describes beautifully the dynamics of absorption. She understands how we constantly talk to ourselves in our heads, analyzing and prying, figuring things out, as you are doing right now reading this book. Unlike most of us, she knows that in this state she will never really "see." She knows that beyond our everyday seeing there is another way of seeing, another way of experiencing, which is all-important. While an effort must be made to see this other way, effort on its own will not succeed. Something else, wholly spontaneous, must happen. Here is her description of being captured by an aspect of nature and connected to what she is seeing:

> It was sunny one evening last summer at Tinker Creek; the sun was low in the sky, upstream. I was sitting on the sycamore log bridge with the sunset at my back, watching the shiners the size of minnows who were feeding over the muddy sand in skittery schools. Again and again, one fish, then the other, turned for a split second across the current and flash! the sun shot out from its silver side. I couldn't watch for

it. It was always just happening somewhere else, and it drew my vision just as it
disappeared: flash, like a sudden dazzle
of the thinnest blade, a sparking over a dun
and olive ground at chance intervals from
every direction. Then I noticed white
specks, some sort of pale petals, small, float-
ing from under my feet on the creek's surface, very slow and steady. So I blurred my
eyes and gazed toward the brim of my hat
and saw a new world. I saw the pale white
circles roll up, roll up, like the world's turn-
ing, mute and perfect, and I saw the linear
flashes, gleaming like silver, like stars being born at random down a rolling scroll
of time. Something broke and something
opened. I filled up like a new wineskin. I
breathed an air like light; I saw a light like
water. I was the lip of a fountain the creek
filled forever; I was ether, the leaf in the
zephyr; I was flesh-flake, feather, bone.

Annie Dillard experiences joy. Captured by the scene,
she is so attentive to it that her inner talk stops on its
own, spontaneously. Then, she softens further and
"something opened." Her body is ready to absorb and
be filled by what she is sensing. She struggles to de-

scribe her indescribable joy. Clearly, she has felt the effects of absorbing a sensory impression, as she wrote elsewhere: "When I walk without a camera, my own shutter opens, and the moment's light prints on my silver gut."

Finally, in two passages from *Walden*, Thoreau states with great precision how he feels as his body absorbs the stimuli here and now:

> This is a delicious evening, when one's whole body is one sense, and imbibes delight through every pore.

~ ~ ~

> Men esteem truth remote, in the outskirts of the system, behind the farthest star, before Adam and after the last man. In eternity there is indeed something true and sublime. But all these times and places and occasions are now and here. God himself culminates in the present moment, and will never be more divine in the lapse of all the ages. And we are enabled to apprehend what is sublime and noble only by the perpetual instilling and drenching of the reality that surrounds us.

I use the word "absorb" to denote the experience variously described as "the moment's light prints on my silver gut," "something opened," and "perpetual instilling and drenching." When our body absorbs an impression, something unique is going on that is qualitatively different from that of our ordinary experiences of the world. We are experiencing the world with our body as well as our mind. The act of the body absorbing a sensory impression is the critical culminating element in the sequence of events that leads to joy. It distinctly separates joy from other positive feelings such as delight and pleasure.

CHAPTER FIVE

A Continuum

WHEN WE THINK of a continuum, it is usually as a seamless progression of entities, with the end of each blending into the beginning of the next so gradually that it is impossible to mark the separations. And that is how I use the term "continuum" when I consider pleasure, delight, and joy as degrees of feeling on a continuum of sensory intensity and involvement. A given positive sensory impression can lead to being pleased, delighted, or joyous.

What makes the difference is the state of the individual encountering the stimulus. That is to say, the person's degree of attentiveness, the extent to which their body is relaxed and softened, and whether it has absorbed the stimulus. At the same time, some sensory impressions certainly are more captivating than others, and more likely to promote a state of attention that will ultimately produce delight or joy. This is how I distinguish the levels of positive feelings on a continuum from pleasure to joy:

- "Being pleased" can be thought of as an ordinary, everyday experience and a function of our typical discursive mind and random attention. One is pleased with the taste of a particularly good meal served with a fine Medoc. Granted, appreciation of the Medoc can be sensory, but usually it is also intellectual when we consider the year and the vineyard, and when we try to label the experience.

- With "delight," our attention is captured by something particularly arresting. The experience is not totally mediated by our mind. Some of the sensory impressions are taken in more directly by the body. As a consequence, the experience is more intense and deeply felt.

- "Joy," at the end of the continuum, is characterized by extraordinary vividness and a whole-mind-body involvement. It seems of a different quality. So much of the sensory impression is taken in directly—absorbed, as it were—that the experience is intense and startling. It feels different. Moreover, because the impressions have been less mediated by the mind, we are less able to make rational sense of the experience.

We are "pleased" by what we primarily perceive with our head. We are "delighted" by what we perceive with both head and senses. However, "joy" results almost exclusively from our sensory impressions. For that reason alone, joy is unique.

Let me give a personal example of experiencing levels of positive feelings on a continuum. In the morning when the day is fair, I like to sit on my front porch where I have a view across the lawn to a pond and a river with marsh on either side. There is distance in this view, there is water, and lots of interesting trees and grasses. To look at this scene is always pleasurable and relaxing for me. Occasionally, I put down my book and just look. If I become captivated by what I am seeing, I pay closer attention to it, my mind quiets down and focuses on the view, and my body begins to relax and soften. When this happens, I experience delight at what I see.

On rare occasions, this process goes a step further. For a moment my body soaks in the sensory impressions of the scene. I feel in my body what I am seeing with my eyes. There are no thoughts. My body and the sensory impressions of the scene are one, inseparable. There is an intimacy, if you will. I feel joy.

Through my readings in literature I have been convinced that pleasure, delight, and joy are levels on a continuum of shared characteristics. And at the pinnacle of the hierarchy is joy. The excerpts below help reveal these distinctions.

Pleasure

In *Huckleberry Finn* by Mark Twain, it seems to me that Huck is expressing simply his general pleasure from days on the river with Jim:

> Two or three days and nights went by; I reckon I might say they swum by, they slid along so quiet and smooth and lovely. Here is the way we put in the time. It was a monstrous big river down there—sometimes a mile and a half wide; we run nights, and laid up and hid daytimes; soon as night was most gone we stopped navigating and

tied up—nearly always in the dead water under a towhead; and then cut young cottonwoods and willows, and hid the raft with them. Then we set out the lines. Next we slid into the river and had a swim, so as to freshen up and cool off; then we set down on the sandy bottom where the water was about knee-deep, and watched the daylight come. Not a sound anywhere's—perfectly still—just like the whole world was asleep, only sometimes the bullfrogs a-cluttering, maybe. The first thing to see, looking away over the water, was a kind of dull line that was the woods on t'other side; you couldn't make nothing else out; then a pale place in the sky; then more paleness spreading around; then the river softened up away off, and warn't black any more, but gray; you could see little dark spots drifting along ever so far away—trading-scows, and such things; and long black streaks—rafts; sometimes you could hear a sweep screaking; or jumbled-up voices, it was so still, and sounds come so far; and by and by you could see a streak on the water which you know by the look of the streak that there's a snag there in a

swift current which breaks on it and makes
that streak look that way; and you see the
mist curl up off of the water, and the east
reddens up, and the river, and you make
out a log cabin in the edge of the woods,
away on the bank on t'other side of the
river, being a wood-yard, likely, and piled
by them cheats so you can throw a dog
through it anywheres; then the nice breeze
springs up, and comes fanning you from
over there, so cool and fresh and sweet to
smell on account of the woods and the
flowers; but sometimes not that way, because they've left dead fish laying around,
gars and such, and they do get pretty rank;
and next you've got the full day, and everything smiling in the sun, and the
song-birds just going it!

Huck describes the pleasure of their ritual when they
stop navigating and tie up. They have a swim to
freshen up and cool off. The sun rises, the world
emerges, then a nice breeze springs up, cool and fresh
and sweet. They have got the full day, and everything
smiling in the sun. His pleasure is full but not neces-
sarily intense; his mind is pleased with what his body
is sensing.

Now here is a passage from John Cheever's *The Wapshot Chronicle,* where Leander, the protagonist of the story, is writing of his youth. As an adult, he is still just as oriented to his senses as when he was young. He has never lost his capacity to be pleased, which is what makes Leander such a charming character:

> Sad tunes sometimes; sometimes gay. Thunderstorms. Christmas. Sounds of fish horn with which writer was called home to supper. Sailed with father on small schooner. Zoe. Moored at river in foot of garden on summer months. High sided; small, counter stem. Short overhang bow. Good cabin with transom and small galley. Thirty-foot water line. Moderate sail plan. Mainsail, foresail, two jibs set on jib-stay. One good-sized. She was dry in rough weather. She moved very well off the wind, quartering it or before it wing and wing, but "on the wind" or "up the wind" as they say today, she moved like real estate. Did not hold at all close going to windward and sagged off badly. Schooner crewed by Daniel Knight. Retired sailor. Old then. About five feet eight. 170 lbs. Broad-beamed and lively. Remembered

> square-riggers, Calcutta, Bombay, China,
> Java. Went out to Zoe in tender. First cer-
> emony on getting aboard was meeting in
> cabin of father and crew. Libation of
> Barkham's rum and molasses. I was not in
> at slicing of mainbrace; but I can smell it
> now. More savory world then, than today.
> Smell of ship's-bread bakery. Green coffee
> beans roasted once a week. Perfumery of
> roasted coffee floated miles downriver.
> Lamp smoke. Smell of cistern water. Lye
> from privy. Wood fires.

Leander is remembering the "savory" world of the past. All the sense impressions he describes were pleasing, and in his memory he is equally pleased. Once again, the experience is more mellow than intense. And, of course, the experience is not direct—it is based on memory.

Delight

Moving up the continuum, as expressed in literature, here is another quote from *Huckleberry Finn* that I believe, in this case, expresses a more intense, involved feeling of delight:

The door of the cavern was big enough to
roll a hogshead in,—and on one side of the
door the floor stuck out a little bit, and was
flat and a good place to build a fire on. So
we built it there and cooked dinner.

We spread the blankets inside for a carpet,
and eat our dinner in there. We put all the
other things handy at the back of the cavern. Pretty soon it darkened up, and begun
to thunder and lighten; so the birds was
right about it. Directly it begun to rain, and
it rained like all fury, too, and I never see
the wind blow so. It was one of these regu-
lar summer storms. It would get so dark
that it looked all blue-black outside, and
lovely; and the rain would thrash along by
so thick that the trees off a little ways
looked dim and spider-webby; and here
would come a blast of wind that would
bend the trees down and turn up the pale
underside of the leaves; and then a perfect
ripper of a gust would follow along and
set the branches to tossing their arms as if
they was just wild; and next, when it was
just about the bluest and blackest—fst! It
was as bright as glory, and you'd have a
little glimpse of treetops a-plunging about

away off yonder in the storm, hundreds of yards further than you could see before; dark as sin again in a second, and now you'd hear the thunder let go with an awful crash, and then go rumbling, grumbling, tumbling, down the sky towards the under side of the world, like rolling empty barrels down-stairs—where it's long stairs and they bounce a good deal, you know. "Jim, this is nice," I says. "I wouldn't want to be nowhere else but here. Pass me along another hunk of fish and some hot corn-bread."

The visual impressions are dynamic and exciting. You can feel Huck's response. He is captivated by it all. He wants to be nowhere else but here. He is experiencing something special, not just another pleasurable day.

Joy

At the peak of the continuum of positive feelings, joy is of a different order. Indeed, as we read in the following passage from Cheever's *The Wapshot Chronicle*, it is a far richer, more profound experience of both mind and body:

The cottage was far away—a place that belonged to Leander's time—a huddle of twelve or sixteen cottages, so awry and weather-faded that they might have seemed thrown up to accommodate the victims of some disaster had you not known that they had been built for those people who make a pilgrimage each summer to the sea. The house they went to was like West Farm, a human burrow or habitation that had yielded at every point to the crotchets and meanderings of a growing family. They put down their bags and undressed for a swim.

It was out of season, early or late, and the inn and the gift shop were under lock and key and they went down the path, hand in hand, as bare as the day they were born with no thought of covering themselves, down the path, dust and in some place ashes and then fine sand like the finest sugar and crusty—it would set your teeth on edge—down onto the coarser sand, wet from the high tide and the sea, ringing then with the music of slammed doors. There was a rock offshore and Betsey swam for this, Coverly following her through the rich, medicinal broths of the North Atlantic. She sat naked on the rock when he approached her, combing her hair with her fingers, and when he climbed up on the rock she dived back into the sea and he followed her to shore.

Then he could have roared with joy, kicked up his heels in a jig and sung a loud tune, but he walked instead along the edge of the sea picking up skimmers and firing them out to beyond the surf where they skittered sometimes and sometimes sank. And then a great sadness of contentment seemed to envelop him—a joy so fine that it gently warmed his skin and bones like the first fires of autumn—and going back to her then, still picking skimmers and firing them, slowly, for there was no rush, and kneeling beside her, he covered her mouth with his and her body with his and then—his body raked and exalted—he seemed to see a searing vision of some golden age that bloomed in his mind until he fell asleep.

When Cheever wrote, "his body raked and exalted— he seemed to see a searing vision of some golden age," he is describing an emotion too powerful, too physical, to be called simple pleasure, or even delight. Clearly it is at the extreme end of the positive feeling continuum, and also a leap beyond. I suggest that Coverly is experiencing joy—with its wealth of characteristics: great intensity, a sense of connectedness, even paradox and contradiction.

As we have seen, distinctions can be drawn between the various levels of positive feelings of pleasure, delight, and joy. Next we will look at the distinguishing characteristics of joy, the most extreme and powerful of these feelings.

CHAPTER SIX

Characteristics of Joy

U P TO THIS point we have been exploring the process or sequence of events that lead to joy. Now let us look at the actual characteristics of this experience and the effects of joy as described in literature. For it is here, in literature, that we read of its complexity and richness, where we can appreciate the efforts of those authors who have tried to describe the indescribable. Luckily for us, many have succeeded brilliantly.

Powerful

Emily Dickinson, for one, captures the extraordinary uniqueness of joy, its magnitude and power:

I can wade Grief—
Whole Pools of it—
I'm used to that—
But the least push of Joy
Breaks my feet—
And I tip—drunken—
Let no Pebble—smile—
T'was the New Liquor—
That was all!

Intense

The joy I am describing in this book is not a form of mysticism, a merging with some form of the Absolute or with another dimension of reality. Rather, it is an intensification of reality, of the sensory world, and a vibrant connection to that physical world. Dickinson describes such intensity when she writes of a mountain man's first experience of going to sea:

Exultation is the going
Of an inland soul to sea,
Past the houses—past the headlands—
Into deep Eternity—
Bred as we, among the mountains,
Can the sailor understand

The divine intoxication
Of the first league out from land?

In *Walden*, Thoreau also writes of this intensification, although he is more concerned with what produces the experience and what the experience implies with regard to how a man should conduct his life:

If the day and the night are such that you meet them with joy, and life emits a fragrance like flowers and sweet-scented herbs, is more elastic, more starry, more immortal—that is your success. All nature is your congratulation, and you have cause momentarily to bless yourself. The greatest gains and values are farthest from being appreciated. We easily come to doubt if they exist. We soon forget them. They are the highest reality. Perhaps the facts most astounding to man and most real are never communicated man to man. The true harvest of my daily life is somewhat as intangible and indescribable as the tints of morning or evening. It is a little stardust caught, a segment of the rainbow which I have clutched.

And in his *Journal*, Thoreau once again portrays the intensity and effects of a joy experience when he writes, "A slight sound at the evening lifts me up by the ears, and makes life seem inexpressibly serene and grand."

Complex

The complexity, richness, brevity of joy seems to tumble out onto the page in *Surprised by Joy* where C. S. Lewis describes it as "seconds of gold scattered in months of dross." Indeed, joy is so enriching that it is like drawing aside a curtain to reveal the heavens. Everyday life pales in comparison to such an extent that one can become sick with desire for more:

> And the world itself—can I have been unhappy, living in Paradise? What keen, tingling sunlight there was! The mere smells were enough to make a man tipsy—cut grass, dew-dabbled mosses, sweet pea, autumn woods, wood burning, peat, salt water. The senses ached. I was sick with desire; that sickness better than health. All this is true, but it does not make the other version a lie. I am telling a story of two lives. They have nothing to do with each other: oil and vinegar, a river running be-

side a canal, Jekyll and Hyde. Fix your eye on either and it claims to be the whole truth. When I remember my outer life I see clearly that the other is but momentary flashes, seconds of gold scattered in months of dross, each instantly swallowed up in the old, familiar, sordid, hopeless weariness. When I remember my inner life I see that everything mentioned in the last two chapters was merely a coarse curtain which at any moment might be drawn aside to reveal all the heavens I then knew.

Fresh

All of the above passages attest to yet another characteristic of the complex feeling of joy—that of a freshness, a newness. It makes sense that the very process leading to joy makes it inevitable. The attention and softening of the organism results in a relaxation of the categorizations we normally impose on experiences, and under these conditions our perceptions are less rigorously processed. This allows for a freshness of perception and the impression is absorbed as such by the body. We absorb the pure energy of the impression, not its preprogrammed label, and we feel it as new and fresh. Our organism now includes that energy, and for a brief moment we are connected and continuous with whatever in the physical world produced that impression.

Fleeting

Joy is but a fleeting moment. This attribute is recognized in almost all literary descriptions of the experience. Here is what the neurologist Antonio Damasio wrote in *Looking for Spinoza: Joy, Sorrow, and the Feeling Brain:*

> For all the courage, perseverance, sacrifices, and discipline necessary to achieve that perfect joy, all one gets are moments of perfection. These are furtive glimpses of what? The divine? The balm is brief and one is left waiting for the next such moment, the next such glimpse. Depending on who you are, this is either bountiful or not nearly enough.

Paradoxical

The characteristics of joy described so far include a great vividness and intensity, a sense of intimacy, a fresh and unique quality—all of this occurring ever so briefly. But there is yet another characteristic that is most intriguing—a paradoxical or contradictory component that is often a part of the joy experience. Cheever's line quoted in the previous chapter, "a great sadness of contentment seemed to envelop him," reflects just such a paradox in a moment of joy.

An explanation for this odd phenomenon is grounded in the process that leads to joy. Percepts and impressions are normally filtered by the mind and thrown into their appropriate category. But, as we know by now, joy is less mediated by the head and more a function of the senses. When one has been attentive and the body has softened, such impressions are less filtered and more directly absorbed. Thus, when sensory impressions are not rationalized and sorted by the mind, they can contain material or information that is at odds with the way the brain normally classifies. As a consequence, these sensory impressions can appear contradictory or paradoxical— with qualities such as the past and present, sadness and contentment, being perceived simultaneously.

Desirable

It is not surprising in the least, once one feels the overwhelming intensity and intimacy of joy with its richness and newness, that one would desire to recapture that feeling. One develops a great yearning for more. C. S. Lewis writes of this in several places in *Surprised by Joy:*

> I will only underline the quality common to the three experiences; it is that of an unsatisfied desire which is itself more desirable than any other satisfaction. I call it joy, which is here a technical term and must be sharply distinguished from Happiness and from Pleasure. Joy (in my sense) has indeed one characteristic, and only one, in common with them; the fact that anyone who has experienced it will want it again. Apart from that, and considered only in its quality, it might almost equally well be called a particular unhappiness or grief. But then it is a kind we want. I doubt whether anyone who has tasted it would ever, if both were in his power, exchange it for all the pleasures in the world. But then joy is never in our power and pleasure often is.

~ ~ ~

> Oh, I desire too much—and before I knew what I desired, the desire itself was gone, the whole glimpse withdrawn, the world

turned commonplace again, or only stirred
by a longing for the longing that had just
ceased.

Yearning for more joy is completely understandable.
But for some it becomes a frustrating, unsatisfied desire.

CHAPTER SEVEN

Recapturing Joy

THERE ARE SOME who would like to believe that the joy experience is the world as it really is, after the mist has been lifted from one's eyes. Its extraordinary quality is, as C. S. Lewis notes, "in another dimension." After a truly joyous experience, one returns to a world that has paled, or as Lewis puts it, "the world turned commonplace again," and "anyone who has experienced it will want it again." Attempting to recapture joy takes many forms.

In *Swann's Way*, Marcel Proust gives perhaps the most detailed description I have encountered of an attempt to recapture joy. When a spoonful of tea sets off an exalted feeling, he drinks a second mouthful, which yields nothing, and a third, which yields even less. He realizes it is "plain that the truth I am seeking is not in the cup but in myself." He examines his mind and seeks to find the truth behind his experience. He describes his elaborate attempt to recapture the initial feeling. Finally, he recognizes he must "leave the thing alone, to drink my tea and to think merely of the worries of today and my hopes for tomorrow, which can be brooded over painlessly":

> Many years had elapsed during which nothing of Combray, except what lay in the theatre and the drama of my going to bed there, had any existence for me, when one day in winter, on my return home, my mother, seeing that I was cold, offered me some tea, a thing I did not ordinarily take. I declined at first, and then, for no particular reason, changed my mind. She sent for one of those squat, plump little cakes called "petites madeleines," which look as though they had been moulded in the fluted valve of a scallop shell. And soon, mechanically, dispirited after a dreary day with the prospect of a depressing morrow, I raised to my lips a spoonful of the tea in which I had soaked a morsel of the cake. No sooner had the warm liquid mixed with

the crumbs touched my palate than a shiver ran through me and I stopped, intent upon the extraordinary thing that was happening to me. An exquisite pleasure had invaded my senses, something isolated, detached, with no suggestion of its origin. And at once the vicissitudes of life had become indifferent to me, its disasters innocuous, its brevity illusory—this new sensation having had the effect, which love has, of filling me with a precious essence; or rather this essence was not in me, it was me. I had ceased now to feel mediocre, contingent, mortal. Whence could it have come to me, this all-powerful joy? I sensed that it was connected with the taste of the tea and the cake, but that it infinitely transcended those savours, could not, indeed, be of the same nature. Where did it come from? What did it mean? How could I seize and apprehend it?

I drink a second mouthful, in which I find nothing more than in the first, then a third, which gives me rather less than the second. It is time to stop; the potion is losing its virtue. It is plain that the truth I am seeking lies not in the cup but in myself. The drink has called it into being, but does not

know it, and can only repeat indefinitely,
with a progressive diminution of strength,
the same message which I cannot interpret,
though I hope at least to be able to call it
forth again and to find it there presently,
intact and at my disposal, for my final enlightenment.

Proust would have welcomed the guidance of Annie
Dillard, who may well provide the model for how to
pursue and recapture the experience of joy. In a passage from *Pilgrim at Tinker Creek*, Dillard gives us clues
and brilliantly describes how to ready oneself for joy:

The secret of seeing is, then, the pearl of
great price. If I thought he could teach
me to find it and keep it forever I would
stagger barefoot across a hundred
deserts after any lunatic at all. But although the pearl may be found, it may
not be sought. The literature reveals this
above all: although it comes to those who
wait for it, it is always, even to the most
practiced and adept, a gift and a total
surprise. I return from one walk knowing where the killdeer nests in the field
by the creek and the hour the laurel

blooms. I return from the same walk a
day later scarcely knowing my own name.
Litanies hum in my ears; my tongue flaps
in my mouth Ailinon alleluia! I cannot
cause light; the most I can do is put myself
in the path of its beam. It is possible, in
deep space, to sail on solar wind. Light, be
it particle or wave, has force: you rig a gi-
ant sail and go. The secret of seeing is to
sail on solar wind. Hone and spread your
spirit till you yourself are a sail, whetted,
translucent, broadside to the nearest puff.

Although the experience of joy is always a gift and a
total surprise, it comes to those who wait in a particular way for it. Think what you are like when you wait:
not waiting in traffic, but waiting expectant of something delightful, the arrival of a person close to you.
You are alert, attentive, tuned into the anticipated
meeting. You are more attentive than usual. I believe
this is what Annie Dillard means when she says that it
comes to those who wait. I believe she confirms the
role of attentiveness and softening when she elo-
quently writes, "Hone and spread your spirit till you
yourself are a sail, whetted, translucent, broadside to
the nearest puff." To hone and spread your spirit is to
become more attentive. To be whetted and translu-

cent is a good description of the softened body. Now put the attentive, softened body broadside to that which may prompt delight, and you have the potential for joy.

Pursuing joy can be a mixed blessing, however, requiring extraordinary fortitude while yielding but the briefest "peep" of brilliance. In his poem "Atlantis," W. H. Auden has his hero give thanks and lay down content after only a mere glimpse of Atlantis:

> Being set on the idea
> Of getting to Atlantis,
> You have discovered of course
> Only the Ship of Fools is
> Making the voyage this year . . .

> Assuming you beach at last
> Near Atlantis, and begin
> The terrible trek inland
> Through squalid woods and frozen
> Tundras where all are soon lost;
> If, forsaken then, you stand,
> Dismissal everywhere,
> Stone and snow, silence and air,
> O remember the great dead
> And honour the fate you are,
> Travelling and tormented,
> Dialectic and bizarre.

Stagger onward rejoicing;
And even then if, perhaps
Having actually got
To the last col, you collapse
With all Atlantis shining
Below you yet you cannot
Descend, you should still be proud
Even to have been allowed
just to peep at Atlantis
In a poetic vision:
Give thanks and lie down in peace,
Having seen your salvation.

Auden's poem gives an account of the journey his hero-seeker undertakes for just one "peep" at Atlantis. To gain that glimpse, the seeker in the poem must make the voyage on the Ship of Fools and weather fierce storms. He must "listen to witty scholars, men who have proved there cannot be such a place as Atlantis," and yet see through what they say. He must learn that sheer doggedness will not get him there, that he must at times be able to forget about Atlantis. And he must learn to see what is counterfeit when "in some bar a tart, as she strokes your hair, should say, 'this is Atlantis, dearie'." Finally, the seeker must make "the terrible trek inland through squalid woods and frozen tundras where all are soon lost," to gain just a "peep" and yet feel it was well worth the arduous journey.

There are those who try to use shortcuts in their pursuit, to no avail. You will remember from an earlier excerpt that E. B. White's character Trexler observed, "when you sauntered along Third Avenue and looked through the doorways into the dim saloons, you could sometimes pick out from the unregenerate ranks the ones who had not forgotten, gazing steadily into the bottom of their glasses on the long chance that they could get another little peek at it." The quest is not only long and demanding; it can lead you astray and yield not "salvation" but despair. Yet feeling true joy is so powerful and compelling that after a single experience, many will want to recapture it.

There are difficulties and barriers to experiencing joy. Being aware of the barriers is critical but not meant to deter. You will find the pursuit can be enriching in and of itself. And occasionally the pursuit may lead you to encounter joy.

CHAPTER EIGHT

Barriers to Joy

JOY HAS BEEN positioned at the extreme end of a continuum that begins with pleasure. A given sensory impression can lead to all levels of positive feeling, with pleasure the most common and joy the least common. Whether one must first be able to experience pleasure and delight in order to experience joy is unclear. But it certainly seems logical that if one is more receptive to pleasure and delight, then one is more likely to experience joy as well. Conversely, if for one reason or another an individual is unable or unlikely to experience pleasure or delight, then that person is not likely to experience much joy either.

There are perhaps many reasons we do not experience more pleasure and delight than we do. Some reasons are quite obvious and understandable: chronic pain, worry, and apprehension are but a few. The list is endless, but I would like to focus on what are in my opinion the three most fundamental and pervasive culprits: unnoticed "little things" and a reluctance to be pleased by them; our hungry imaginations; and our common state of information-processing or focused goal-orientation. All of these factors contribute to the overarching difficulty of not being attentive or present. These barriers are not discrete factors but, rather, are interrelated in the way they affect our lives.

Awareness of these barriers is the first step in surmounting them, if one so desires. As Daido Roshi succinctly puts it, "The moment is where our life takes place. If we miss the moment we miss our life." Since joy occurs only in the present, let us examine some of the barriers and reasons we are not present to our life.

Things Unnoticed

There are two aspects of this barrier: failure to notice the little ordinary things we encounter each day, and then, even if we do notice, we may just refuse or be reluctant to be pleased by them. To elucidate, I will draw on the English writer, essayist, and moralist Samuel Johnson, who lived from 1709 to 1784. For much of his life, Johnson was unrecognized and poor. The search for psychological stability and happiness was a constant theme in his life. But in his search for happiness, he was an ardent realist. In *The Rambler, No. 68*, he wrote:

> The main of life is, indeed, composed of small incidents and petty occurrences; of wishes for objects not remote, and grief for disappointments of no fatal consequence; of insect vexations which sting us and fly away, impertinences, which buzz awhile about us, and are heard no more; of meteorous pleasures which dance before us and are dissipated; of compliments which glide off the soul like other musick, and are forgotten by him that gave, and him that received them.
>
> Such is the general heap out of which every man is to cull his own condition: for, as the chemists tell us, that all bodies are resolvable into the same elements, and that the boundless variety of things arises from the different proportions of very few ingre-

dients; so a few pains and a few pleasures are all the materials of human life, and of these the proportions are partly allotted by Providence, and partly left to the arrangement of reason and of choice.

As these are well or ill disposed, man is for the most part happy or miserable. For very few are involved in great events, or have their thread of life entwisted with the chain of causes on which armies or nations are suspended; and even those who seem wholly busied in publick affairs, and elevated above low cares, or trivial pleasures, pass the chief part of their time in familiar and domestick scenes; from these they came into publick life, to these they are every hour recalled by passions not to be suppressed; in these they have the reward of their toils, and to these at last they retire.

The great end of prudence is to give cheerfulness to those hours, which splendour cannot gild, and acclamation cannot exhilarate; those soft intervals of unbended amusement, in which a man shrinks to his natural dimensions, and throws aside the ornaments or disguises, which he feels in privacy to be useless encumbrances, and which lose all effect when they become familiar. To be happy at home is the ultimate result of all ambition, the end to which every enterprise and labour tends, and of which every desire prompts the prosecution.

To be happy at home and with the little things of life should be our ambition, but probably this is not often the case. We go after the big things in life, particularly those things that are significant in the view of others. Isn't it interesting how many of the little things in life fail to please us? I walk out the door on a warm and brilliantly sunny day and proceed to my car without even looking up, totally absorbed in what I need to accomplish. I do not stop for even five seconds to enjoy the warmth and to be pleased by the play of light on the grass. Thoreau, in his *Journal*, encourages us to be alert and look:

> But while we are confined to books, though the most select and classic, and read only particular written languages, which are themselves but dialects and provincial, we are in danger of forgetting the language which all things and events speak without metaphor, which alone is copious and

standard. Much is published but little printed. The rays which stream through the shutter will no longer be remembered when the shutter is wholly removed. No method or discipline can supersede the necessity of forever being alert. What is a course of history, or philosophy, or poetry, no matter how well selected, or the best society, or the most admirable routine of life, compared with the discipline of looking always at what is to be seen? Will you be a reader, a student merely, or a seer? Read your fate, see what is before you, and walk into futurity.

Why we normally do not look and see is a whole other subject. What is relevant to our concern here is that, even when we do turn to the small things in life, we often do not find delight in them. According to Johnson, this is because of an almost active predisposition—we refuse to be pleased. And we refuse to be pleased because of the demands and expectations we place on life. There are many reasons we do this to ourselves. Perhaps we feel we are owed something because we missed out on it in the past, or we expect as much of something that we perceive others have. As a consequence, when a small something comes

along, we are not pleased with it. Think hard for a
moment of how you expect to be treated by the people
you love. It is hard to take delight in what they offer
if you expect a lot more.

In a word, we can choose to be disappointed by
the little things that life delivers us on a daily basis or
we can choose to be pleased by them. If we choose to
be pleased, we will surely be delighted on some occasions and we might even experience joy. In any event,
noticing means we are present, and this puts us in the
right place for joy.

Hungry Imagination

In addition to our inattentiveness to little everyday
things, there is another explanation for why we seldom live wholly in the present. Samuel Johnson, who
was interested in our inability to be in the present,
blamed it on the "hunger of our imagination." W. Jackson Bates, the definitive contemporary biographer of
Samuel Johnson, has this to say about Johnson's thinking on the subject:

> The "hunger of imagination" puts in a
> strong metaphor a perception that per-
> vades Johnson's moral writing: that "so

few of the hours of life are filled up with
objects adequate to the mind of man"—
which can conceive and therefore want so
much more than any moment of the present
can ever supply—"that we are forced to
have recourse every moment to the past and
future for supplemental satisfactions."
Scarcely an hour passes that we are not
looking ahead to the next hour, the next
day, the next week, or looking back in the
same way. "No mind is much employed
upon the present: recollection and anticipation fill up almost all our moments."
Time and again, in making excuses for
human nature, he would recur to this observation, as Mrs. Thrale noticed. The
phrases appear on every page: we are
forced to "relieve the vacuities of our being
by recollection . . . or anticipation of events
to come"; riches fail to "fill up the vacuities of life"; the attempts of visitors at summer resorts to "rid themselves of the day";
literary quarreling for many people "re-
lieves the vacancies of life."

The fantasies we create in our minds to entertain ourselves while we undertake the mundane tasks of life

are appealing. Who wants to attend to doing the dishes or washing the car? How much more enticing it is to drift off into thought or fantasy and envision sailing in the Mediterranean.

On a broader scale, we may go so far as to create in our minds a story about our lives with all the characteristics of a good novel. With heroes and villains, suspense and adventure, the creation and elaboration of our story, our life, is not only pleasurable but also very meaningful to us. If our story is one of rags to riches, the meaning this provides in our culture is obvious. Even if our story is one of squandered possibilities, it can still be a good story full of surprises, high drama, and dash. Why would one want to give up this self-created life to be present and attentive to cutting the grass or to the other humdrum events of daily life? Well, the reason would be—to be present and experience one's *actual* unfolding life, where there is always the potential to experience joy.

Information-Processing

Another more profound and fundamental reason we are rarely present to a current situation is that we constantly process incoming sensory data. We do this because we are often focused on a goal or want to solve a problem. This common characteristic, however, is a barrier to joy as it rarely occurs to us to focus on input for its own sake.

Let me share a recent experience to help describe this most difficult barrier to joy. One morning I was taking a walk on the beach in Bucerias, Mexico. I was on vacation, and it was going to be a long, unhurried walk. I was alone and had nothing in particular to think about. It was yet another clear, warm, sunny day. I decided I would attend to the experience of what I was seeing, sensing, and hearing. I was intensely conscious of the light on the water, the sound of the surf, the feeling of the sand on the bottom of my feet. Because I was attending so exclusively to my surroundings, I was to a very large extent in the present, and while I did not experience joy, I certainly felt a great delight.

I was carrying my sandals, and when I stopped to turn around and walk back, I discovered that I had dropped one somewhere along the beach. As the tide was going out, there was a good chance I would be able to find it. It could be washing about at the water's edge, or someone might have thrown it further up the beach so it would not be washed away. As a consequence, I began to scan a fairly wide area of beach for any sign of my sandal. I was acutely aware of my visual field of the beach and anything in that field that might be my sandal. As I saw things in the distance that might be my sandal, I had to make constant judgments as to whether I should go closer to investigate or whether I should dismiss that object as a possibility.

In the course of all this information-processing, I suddenly became aware of myself scanning, judging, gathering data, making decisions. All of this was in an attempt to solve the problem of the missing sandal. I was no longer experiencing my surroundings with delight. My world had shrunk from the rich universe of the first part of my walk. I decided to see if I could regain that original experience while at the same time keeping an eye out for my sandal. I could not, even after repeated attempts. I was locked into processing the content of my surroundings, and no longer attending to the light, or the sound, or the feel of the sand. I was instead firmly focused on the visual information I needed to find my sandal (which I eventually did locate).

From this story, you can see how being present means being attentive to an experience for its own sake, with no purpose in mind, no links to something past or anticipated in the future. Too often, however, our most prevalent mode is to gather information from our senses and to use that information to solve a problem or reach a goal. This is not surprising, since our sensory systems evolved to solve problems. When we are attending intellectually to the meaning and implications of an experience, it is not possible to embrace the actual experience itself. If we are almost always fully immersed in understanding and codifying our experience, then there is no part of us remaining to be aware of anything outside that state. And this is why it is so difficult to be present.

An additional factor that is operating when we are focused on a goal or trying to solve a problem is that our bodies are almost always poised for action. As a consequence, our bodies have a degree of tension, perhaps not in the sense that we normally use the word (a tense back or shoulders), but tense in the way a cat is tense right before it pounces on a mouse. In my beach experience, I think it very likely that, once I began looking for my sandal, my body shifted into a state of being poised for action and, apart from my focused scanning of the beach for the sandal, was not available to experience other sense impressions fully, or at all. What I referred to earlier as the absorbing of sense impressions is in fact the ability to experience sense impressions in the body, and this can only occur when the body is softened, not tensed for action. When an individual is in a state of non-goal-oriented receptive attention, she or he can experience simply and directly what takes place in the present without evaluating, analyzing, or trying to understand.

While it is true that processing information to solve a problem or reach a goal will usually preclude experiencing joy, there are situations in which this is not the case. When one is skilled in an activity that requires the use of information in order to perform the activity, it is possible to absorb an experience and still maintain an overall awareness of one's activity. Let me explain, using the experience of sailing a boat, one of my lifelong sources of pleasure.

Properly set, the sail of a boat has the same shape as the wing of an airplane. The force that keeps a plane aloft is the same force that drives a sailboat forward, when the wind is ahead of the boat. Let us say that the wind is coming from the north and that I want to sail in that direction. I have to sail about forty-five degrees to either the right or the left of the wind. If I steer too close to north, the sails will luff and the boat will stop. If I sail too far to the right or left, I defeat my purpose, which is to go north. There is a kind of "groove" at about forty-five degrees off the wind in which the boat is going as fast as possible and as close to north as possible. The challenge is to stay in that groove.

Today, there are instruments that can be viewed from the wheel of the boat that give all the information you need to stay in the groove. One instrument gives the speed through the water. Another gives the angle of the boat's direction to the direction of the wind. You simply find the angle that gives you the greatest speed while going as close to the wind as possible. Then there are telltales on the sails to show how the wind is moving over the sails. If a telltale flutters, you correct your course.

But, in truth, you do not really need all that visual information generated by instruments. You can close your eyes and sail just as well. There are other sources of information. One is the sound of the boat moving through the water. Another is the heeling or leaning over of the boat. There is the motion of the boat, which changes as the direction of the boat changes. And then there is the sound of the wind passing over the sails. There are probably other more subtle cues that provide useful information of which I am not even aware. The result of all these cues is that your body knows when you are in the groove, and it knows immediately when you have lost it. With a little experience, your body knows exactly what to do to get back in the groove. You do not have to think about it. Your hand turns the wheel just the right amount.

Sailing a boat on a fine day in a good breeze is always wonderful. Sailing upwind and using my body to get into the groove and stay there is a source of great delight. I must be quiet and attentive to my body to feel all the relevant sensations fully. True, I am using those sensations as a source of information about how to sail the boat, but after years of sailing this becomes automatic. The wind direction changes, and my hand turns the wheel without having to process any information consciously. Now I have the boat in the groove, I am attentive and present, and it is possible to attend to the sensations for their own sake. The conditions have been established that can lead and have often led to a joyous experience.

So, it seems very possible for one to attend deeply to an experience, in addition to using it as a source of information, as long as the information-processing is relatively automatic. For example, I have never ridden a horse, but I am sure there is a wide variety of sensory cues that riders use to prompt their own movements. If I were learning to ride a horse, I would no doubt have to be so attentive to the information provided by the relevant sensations that I could not attend to the experience of the sensations themselves. But after a while, all this would become automatic, and I could just enjoy the movement of the horse and my own movement in response. There are situations in which you need not be exclusively attentive to what you are experiencing for its own sake in order to be present.

CHAPTER NINE

Cultivating Joy

A FTER READING ABOUT the barriers to being present
and experiencing joy, you can perhaps understand why cultivating joy is such a challenge. However, from personal experience, I know that meeting
the challenge is well worth the effort. The basic re-
quirements for experiencing delight and joy are to be
both present and attentive to sensory experience for
its own sake. When we are truly present and attentive, we soften and absorb more fully the sensory impressions of the moment.

While there is much admonition given these days
to "live in the present" or "be in the moment," probably no one can do so on a sustained basis. There are

really only *moments* in the present, as anyone proficient in meditation will testify. Let me describe what I have experienced in meditating, which can be thought of as practice for living in the present.

I sit down to meditate. I try to focus on my breath or body, and this is the first difficulty, at least until my internal dialogue quiets down. Even then, I do not stay fixed in the present with a focused attention on my breath or body. Rather, I am there for a moment, then I slip away into a thought or sensation. After actively dismissing intrusive thoughts or sensations, I return to my breath or body for another moment, perhaps longer this time. This weaving back and forth continues until at some point, and after years of meditating, it becomes far less of an effort. A person advanced in meditation finds that the present, its slipping away and returning, becomes a kind of organic pulse that repeats without effort. At some point I do not have to remember to come back to myself. But then after a while I start to get tired, and it becomes an effort again. Soon, it is time to stop and enter the day.

When the demands of the day take over, I am so involved in them I forget that I want to be present. The force that for a while during meditation kept bringing me back to myself in the present is no longer there or at least is too weak to compete with the day's activities. Immersed in the events of the day, I am fo-cused on the content of my experience, and use that information to go about the business of my life.

The reality is that you only need to come back to yourself and be present for a moment. Since we are not usually even aware that we are not present, this is most difficult—first, to be aware of yourself in your surroundings and then to remind yourself to be present and attend to your sensory experience for its own sake. But the challenge is to cultivate the habit of doing so again and again.

How does one do this? First, stop and notice. I am dictating this chapter right now while sitting on my porch in the sun on a chilly April day. I am wearing a coat and will have to put on gloves shortly, but I occa-sionally stop dictating to take delight in the warmth of the sun on my shoulders and neck and in the play of light before me. It is a small first step to actually stop and look at the little things in your life that can be pleasing but that you either take for granted or simply ignore. Make it a habit. Choose to notice—choose to be pleased.

Here are a couple of examples from my own life of such conscious choices. The first thing I do when I get up in the morning is to make myself a cup of tea. I happen to like English Breakfast Tea. I drink it while thinking through the day and getting organized. As a result, I never even taste the tea. But with each sip it is possible to stop my mental planning and actually taste the flavor of the tea. The taste can be a real source of pleasure, if I but notice it.

Here is another example. My wife and I live in an old house, which has lovely spaces that seem to flow from room to room very gracefully. I spend an increasing amount of time walking around the house trying to find things that I have misplaced. Usually I am irritated at having lost whatever it is and frustrated at not being able to find it. What a wasted opportunity. I do not even see where I am walking or any of the interesting aspects of our home. However, if I remind myself to look around and enjoy what I see while I'm searching, it makes all the difference in the world.

Let us take a look at some things you can practice to help bring you into the present, improve your attentiveness, and thus make you more available for joy. You are probably thinking, "That's all very well and good, but when do I have the time to do this stuff?" No doubt valid, but you can make time in the following way. Earlier I wrote about how we spend so much time fantasizing the future, reviewing the past, and constructing our story. It is hard to give these things up. They are pleasant and often meaningful. I have not, however, discussed how much time we spend strategizing our day, planning, getting our ducks in a row. Some of this has to be done, but we tend to overdo it. Strategize your day, and then stop. Use the time you save to do the following exercises.

Sit down in a chair and relax. Close your eyes for thirty seconds or a minute. Open them very slowly and look around you slowly, quietly, and receptively. See what is there. Then say to yourself, "I am alive." Then feel it. Feel the miracle that you are living right now. When you stop for a moment and really *feel* that you are in the midst of this world, right now, it can have a profound impact. You suddenly realize that you are really here. It is one thing to know this with your head. It is another to experience it.

As another exercise, take a little chunk of time, let's say one to three minutes, and do nothing. Just look, listen, smell, and touch. This is a kind of variation on the previous exercise. It has the added advantage of generating some evidence that, if you do nothing, the world will not end. Indeed, like the previous exercise, you will suddenly realize that the world is there and that you are a part of it.

Finally, take a new and fresh look at your everyday surroundings. What do they really look like? How do they really sound or smell?

In her novel *Bel Canto*, Ann Patchett wrote about the vice president of an unnamed Latin American country who has for four months been confined inside his house by rebels. Finally, he is allowed to walk out into his yard:

> Vice President Ruben Iglesias, who thought he would not live to feel once again the sensation of grass beneath his feet, stepped off the shale stone walkway and sank into the luxury of his own yard. He had stared at it every day from the living-room window but now that he was actually there it seemed like a new world. Had he ever walked around his own lawn in the evening? Had he made a mental note of the trees, the miraculous flowering bushes that grew up around the wall? What were they called? He dropped his face into the nest of deep purple blossoms and inhaled. Dear God, if he were to get out of this alive he would be attentive to his plants. Maybe he would work as a gardener. The new leaves were bright green and velvety to touch. He stroked them between his thumb and forefinger, careful not to bruise. Too many evenings he had come home after dark. He saw the life in his garden as a series of shadows and silhouettes. If there was ever such a thing as a second chance

he would have his coffee outside in the morning. He would come home to have lunch with his wife in the afternoons on a blanket beneath the trees. His two girls would be in school, but he would hold his son on his knees and teach him the names of birds. How had he come to live in such a beautiful place?

This is what it means to see the world afresh. It is difficult under normal circumstances, but if you try from time to time, you will increasingly appreciate this new habit and enjoy with what you find.

More often than not, joy is a gift. It comes out of nowhere, unexpectedly. But it has been my experience that this gift will come more freely and more fully with a little preparatory effort, but not the kind of effort you put into your career. Rather, it is the kind of effort it takes to do nothing. A "letting go" rather than a "doing." It takes giving up the active pursuit of a goal for a little while and becoming solely an organ of perception. With this change, the world changes, and more joy is often a quality of this changed world.

Moreover, I believe that experiencing joy has a cumulative impact on one's life. Actually, it is not just the accumulation of such experiences. It is the long-term effects of the repeated overall process of being more attentive and softening that, over time, change how we feel, how we think, and how we move. Our entire physical and psychological structure softens. We become more flexible and open in general. We are less dominated and determined by our psychological structure. We are the same person but with greater freedom to respond appropriately to situations, rather than react automatically.

Consider this metaphor: imagine a newborn baby's body as pure, flowing energy. As the baby develops into a person, some of that energy crystallizes into a set of internal psychological structures, which we can call the child's personality. As the child grows older, these structures become more elaborate. They also become harder and less malleable. In time, all the original, flowing energy becomes crystallized into an adult "structure" or habitual ways of reacting.

Western psychology views psychological problems as stemming from this structure and being either at odds with itself or inadequate to deal with the world. Therapeutic practices aim to address the part of the structure that is dysfunctional and attempt to change it. In contrast, there are Eastern schools of psychology that do not attempt to change anything. Their sole approach is to guide the individual in ways to soften, or decrystallize, the entire structure. When the psychological structure has been softened, when it is more open and receptive, then conflicts disappear. The intent is not change but, rather, transformation. People who meditate will attest to the fact that, over time, a softening of their body and psychological structure occurs. I believe that, similarly, the cumulative effect over time of experiencing delight and joy can change our psychological structure.

In the final analysis, I do not know the actual cause or causes of joy, nor to what, in scientific terminology, joy can be reduced. I still do not know what joy tells us about human nature or the nature of reality. What I do believe is that the changes that lead to joy are dimensions of our human nature, and that they are not generally recognized or understood in Western psychology. An understanding of these dimensions or phenomena would provide a fuller conception of ourselves and of our potential for having more enriching experiences. Personally, this exploration has given me a richer comprehension of the possibilities inherent in our natures.

CHAPTER TEN

Intimacy with the World

M YSTICAL JOY USUALLY refers to a union with God
or the cosmos, whereas the joy I have explored
is a feeling prompted by a specific sensory input. However, it does contain an element of mystical union, al-
beit on a limited scale. It gives us a glimpse of the
possibilities for a connectedness on a grander scale. I
would suggest that joy reveals to us our potential to
experience the mystical.

Clearly, the way we perceive the world in our everyday discursive, fragmented, inattentive state is not
the only way. Granted, our normal, everyday habit of
being preoccupied with information-processing is one

that evolved to enhance our survival. But we also have the potential for mindfulness and presence. In an attentive state, we think more flexibly and are able to feel more fully with our entire organism; the preconceived concepts we use to understand the world become less rigid and excluding. We gain a broader perspective and are more receptive to the context of a situation. We see what is actually there, rather than what is dictated by our preconceived categories and conditioning. We are open to new ways of understanding a person or an issue. We are able to feel something directly rather than reacting categorically. We can feel fully with our mind and body. A more general way of saying all of this is that the quality or degree of our attention creates in us a different state of being. This state of awareness, rarely realized, is a very real potential of our human nature.

It is for the above reasons that attention is central to most of the great spiritual traditions. It is a common denominator in many forms of meditation and prayer since, in an attentive state, one is available to an expanded range of experiences beyond the everyday. Meditation practice is an attempt to quiet the mind through concentrated attention on a mantra, the flow of breath, or some object, as the beginning step toward a more pervasive state of pure attention.

The importance of developing attention is most readily seen in the religions of Hinduism and Buddhism. The Hindu system of philosophical meditation, yoga, has as its essential discipline a one-pointed attention or concentration designed to effect reunion with the universal spirit. The different schools of Buddhism emphasize various forms of meditation; but in all, supportive techniques are employed by beginners to collect and focus the mind on a single object in order to quiet mental activity. In the Zen tradition, the practice of zazen leads to either that of shikantaza—an advanced practice without a focus, "just sitting," characterized by intense, nondiscursive awareness, or koan practice—a concentrated form of zazen in which one meditates on a spiritual question and in the course of seeing into this moves deeper into a realization of nonduality. In this way, one reaches samadhi, a nondualistic state of consciousness and awareness where mind and environment are one. Unwavering, vigorous attention, practiced by all Buddhists, is deemed a precondition for one's self-realization, enlightenment, and clear insight into the true nature of the world.

The role of attention is not nearly as central in the three major monotheistic religions, unless we look to their more mystical traditions. Within Islam, Sufism has long required uncompromised concentration of one's attention upon God to create a "unity of attention." The Jewish Kabbalists use mantra-like repetitions of sacred liturgical words as an attentive form of prayer believed to be capable of inducing an altered and higher state of consciousness. Within both Eastern and Western Christianity, there is a long tradition of meditative prayer to open oneself to the divine presence. For example, in the *Philokalia*, written between the fourth and fifteenth centuries by spiritual masters of the Orthodox Christian church, the role of attention is noted in the first essay by Saint Isaiah the Solitary:

> A monk should consider the purpose of each text in Scripture, to whom it speaks and on what occasions. He should persevere continually in the ascetic struggle and be on his guard against the provocations of the enemy. Like a pilot steering a boat through the waves, he should hold to his course, guided by grace. Keeping his attention fixed within himself, he should commune with God in stillness, guarding his thoughts from distraction and his intellect from curiosity.

Outside of the religious context, both G. I. Gurdjieff and Jiddu Krishnamurti taught forms of attention, which they called "self-remembering" and "choiceless awareness," respectively. Both practices are an attempt to develop undistracted, sustained, nonreactive attention to both inner thought and outer activity. The aim is to experience life—not what has happened or will happen, but what is immediate in this very moment.

Through these religious practices and spiritual pursuits, one attempts to achieve union or connectedness with a greater entity, be it God, a universal spirit, the cosmos, or reality. In order to even begin to do so, these traditions emphasize, in varying degrees, the importance of cultivating attention. It is believed that the resulting quiet mind allows for a psychological transformation that can make truth and reality more accessible. The literature, both past and present, of all the major religions confirms this. However, what has not been identified and confirmed is the actual physical change that occurs while in a nonreactive state of attention.

I doubt anyone will ever be able to describe completely the physical dynamics of a full-blown religious or cosmic mystical experience, but some have attempted to describe its characteristics. Evelyn Underhill, in *Mysticism*, wrote of the history and manifestation of the mystic experience within the context of Western Christianity. She documents her study with material drawn from some of the great Christian mystics. A much broader study by Dr. Richard Bucke in *Cosmic Consciousness* looks at mystical experiences and "illumination" across all times, cultures, and religions. His survey ranges from Siddhartha Gautama the Buddha, Jesus, and Mohammed to Dante, Blake, and Whitman, and he attempts to extract the common features of their experience. Two characteristics he identifies are of particular relevance to the nature of joy. All those he studied reported feeling a oneness or connectedness with the universe and described the universe as a "living presence." This feeling is similar to that of joy, where there is a oneness and an aliveness with something particular in the world but not the whole universe.

What I have attempted to describe is the *physical* process of joy that can occur when we are attentive to a specific stimulus. The ultimate effect of the process of softening and absorption is that a discrete part of our world (a musical passage, a lover's body, the sun's last rays on a tree) comes alive. This need not, however, be an innately pleasant aspect of the world. In *Corelli's Mandolin,* Louis De Bernieres wrote of a Greek soldier's experience one night as he fought against an invading Italian army in WWII. The soldier is powerfully impacted by what he sees—he feels the energy of the world in a moment of warfare.

> Once, near the Metsovon pass, in December, when it was twenty degrees below zero

because there was no cloud, the Italians
sent up a starshell. It exploded in a cas-
cade of brilliant blue light against the face
of the full moon, and the sparks drifted to
earth in slow motion like the souls of reluctant angels. As that small magnesium
sun hovered and blazed, the black pines
stepped out of their modest shadows as
though previously they had been veiled like
virgins but had now decided to be seen as
they are in heaven. The drifts of snow
pulsed with the incandescence of the absolute chastity of ice, a mortar coughed dis-
consolately, and an owl whooped. For the
first time in my life I shivered physically
from something other than the cold; the
world had sloughed away its skin and re-
vealed itself as energy and light.

It is my wish to get well so that I can go
back to the lines and experience, perhaps
for only one more time, that immaculate
moment when I saw the face of Gabriel in
an instrument of war.

For that brief moment he felt filled with the life,
energy, and spirit of a distinct aspect of the world as
we do when experiencing joy. We absorb that aspect

into our body, as well as our mind. We are totally connected with its aliveness and are a part of it. No longer
do we feel separated from that part of the world. It is
in us. We, too, are alive with its energy.

This experience of aliveness and intimacy is powerful, enriching, and clearly an end in itself. But it is
also an intimation that life, our life, can be more than
we know in our ordinary state of mind or being. This
intimation—that there is something more to reality
than our everyday awareness or consciousness reveals—is an important aspect of joy. It moves joy beyond being a positive and desirable feeling in and of
itself. As the French poet, Paul Eluard, once wrote,
"There is another world, and it is in this one." Joy
gives us a glimpse of this other world.

BIBLIOGRAPHY

Auden, W. H. *The Collected Poetry of W. H. Auden.* New York: Random House, 1945.

Bate, W. Jackson. *Samuel Johnson.* New York: Harcourt Brace Jovanovich, 1977.

Bucke, Richard Maurice. *Cosmic Consciousness: A Study in the Evolution of the Human Mind.* New York: Dutton, 1969.

Chalmers, David J. *The Conscious Mind: In Search of a Fundamental Theory.* New York: Oxford University Press, 1996.

Cheever, John. *The Wapshot Chronicle.* New York: Harper & Row, 1957.

Chuang-Tzu. *The Seven Inner Chapters and Other Writings from the Book Chuang-Tzu.* Translated by A. C. Graham. London: Allen & Unwin, 1981.

Csikszentmihalyi, Mihaly. *Flow: The Psychology of Optimal Experience.* New York: Harper & Row, 1990.

Damasio, Antonio R. *Descartes' Error: Emotion, Reason, and the Human Brain.* New York: G. P. Putnam, 1994.

———. *The Feeling of What Happens: Body and Emotion in the Making of Consciousness.* New York: Harcourt, 1999.

———. *Looking for Spinoza: Joy, Sorrow, and the Feeling Brain.* New York: Harcourt, 2003.

De Bernieres, Louis. *Corelli's Mandolin.* New York: Random House, 1994.

Dillard, Annie. *Three by Annie Dillard: Pilgrim at Tinker Creek, An American Childhood, The Writing Life.* New York: HarperPerennial, 1990.

Izutsu, Toshihiko. *Sufism and Taoism: A Comparative Study of Key Philosophical Concepts.* Berkeley and Los Angeles: University of California Press, 1984.

James, William. *The Varieties of Religious Experience: A Study in Human Nature.* New York: Modern Library, 1999.

Johnson, Samuel. "*The Rambler No. 68,* Saturday, November 10, 1750." In *The Works of Samuel Johnson in Sixteen Volumes.* Electronic Text Center, University of Virginia Library.

Johnson, Thomas H., ed. *The Complete Poems of Emily Dickinson.* Boston: Little, Brown, 1960.

Kahneman, Daniel, Ed Diener, Norbert Schwarz, eds. *Well-Being: The Foundations of Hedonic Psychology.* New York: Russell Sage Foundation, 1999.

Lewis, C. S. *Surprised by Joy: The Shape of My Early Life.* New York: Harcourt Brace, 1955.

Lewis, Michael, and Jeannette M. Haviland-Jones, eds. *Handbook of Emotions*. New York: Guilford Press, 2000.

Loori, John Daido. *The Still Point*. Mt. Tremper, N.Y.: Dharma Communications, 1996.

Loori, John Daido, ed. *The Art of Just Sitting: Essential Writings on the Zen Practice of Shikantaza*. Boston: Wisdom, 2002.

Maezumi, Taizan. *Appreciate Your Life: The Essence of Zen Practice*. Boston: Shambala, 2001.

Maslow, Abraham H. *Toward a Psychology of Being*. New York: John Wiley & Sons, 1968.

Melville, Herman. *Moby Dick*. New York: Modern Library, 1930.

Merleau-Ponty, Maurice. *"The Primacy of Perception" and Other Essays on Phenomenological Psychology, the Philosophy of Art, History, and Politics*. Edited and with introduction by James M. Edie. Evanston: Northwestern University Press, 1964.

Nasr, Seyyed Hossein. *Knowledge and the Sacred*. New York: Crossroad Publishing, 1981.

Needleman, Jacob, and George Baker, eds. *Gurdjieff: Essays and Reflections on the Man and His Teaching*. New York: Continuum, 1996.

Novak, Philip. "Attention." In *The Encyclopedia of Religion*. New York: Simon & Schuster Macmillan, 1995.

Pashler, Harold E. *The Psychology of Attention*. Cambridge: MIT Press, 1999.

Patchett, Ann. *Bel Canto.* New York: HarperCollins, 2001.

Proust, Marcel. *In Search of Lost Time.* Volume 1 of *Swann's Way.* Translated by C. K. Scott Moncrieff and Terence Kilmartin. New York: Modern Library, 1992.

Rilke, Rainer Maria. *Selected Works: Poetry.* Translated by J. B. Leishman. New York: New Directions, 1967.

Saint Isaiah the Solitary. "On Guarding the Intellect." In *The Philokalia: The Complete Text Compiled by St Nikodimos of the Holy Mountain and St Makarios of Corinth.* Volume 1. Translated and edited by G. E. H. Palmer, Philip Sherrard, and Kallistos Ware. London: Faber & Faber, 1979.

Seligman, Martin E. P. *Authentic Happiness: Using the New Positive Psychology to Realize Your Potential for Lasting Fulfillment.* New York: Free Press, 2000.

Shakespeare, William. *The Merchant of Venice.* Oxford: Oxford University Press, 1993.

Thoreau, Henry D. *Walden and Resistance to Civil Government: Authoritative Texts, Journal, Reviews, and Essays in Criticism.* Edited by William Rossi. New York: Norton, 1992.

Twain, Mark. *Adventures of Huckleberry Finn: Authoritative Text, Contexts, and Sources Criticism.* Edited by Thomas Cooley. New York: Norton, 1999.

Underhill, Evelyn. *Mysticism.* New York: Meridian Books, 1955.

White, E. B. *The Second Tree from the Corner.* New York: HarperPerennial, 1978.

ABOUT THE AUTHOR

A LEXANDER B. PLATT is a management psychologist who has consulted with the senior executives of major corporations for over twenty-five years. Before that he was a dean at Columbia University and a publishing executive. Insights gained from his profession as a psychologist, a practice of meditation, and a lifelong exploration of literature are synthesized in his study of joy.

Dr. Platt is an avid sailor and eclectic reader. He lives with his wife in Connecticut. This is his first book.

Readers may contact the author at aplatt30@aol.com.